chic & simple
SEWING

To shorten, fold on this line
Pour raccourcir, pliez sur cette ligne
Para acortar, dóblese en esta línea

Tuck-dart
Pince-pli
Cuchillo-alforza

chic & simple
SEWING

Skirts, Dresses, Tops, and Jackets for the Modern Seamstress

Christine Haynes

POTTER
CRAFT

NEW YORK

Published in the United States by Potter Craft, an imprint of the Crown Publishing Group,

a division of Random House, Inc., New York.

www.crownpublishing.com

wwww.pottercraft.com

POTTER CRAFT and colophon is a registered trademark of Random House, Inc.

Library of Congress Cataloging-in-Publication Data

Haynes, Christine.

   Chic & Simple Sewing : skirts, dresses, tops, and jackets for the modern seamstress /

Christine Haynes.

     p. cm.

   Includes index.

   ISBN 978-0-307-45109-5

   (1. Sewing.)   I. Title.

   TT705.H39 2009

   646'.1   dc22   2008019456

Printed in China

DESIGN Amy Sly
PHOTO ILLUSTRATIONS Amy Sly
PHOTOGRAPHY Stuart Mullenberg
ILLUSTRATIONS Rena Leinberger
MODELS Annabelle Waters,
Liz Russo, and Tessa Young
MAKEUP Tessa Young

10 9 8 7 6 5 4 3 2 1
First Edition

POTTER CRAFT NEWSLETTER
Sign up for our monthly newsletter at www.pottercraft.com
to get information about new books, receive free patterns,
and enter contests to win prizes.

LOCATIONS USED IN THE PHOTOGRAPHS
MATRUSHKA
3822 West Sunset Boulevard, Los Angeles, CA 90026
323-665-4513
www.Matrushka.com

FORD'S FILLING STATION
9531 Culver Boulevard, Culver City, CA 90232
310-202-1470
www.FordsFillingStation.net

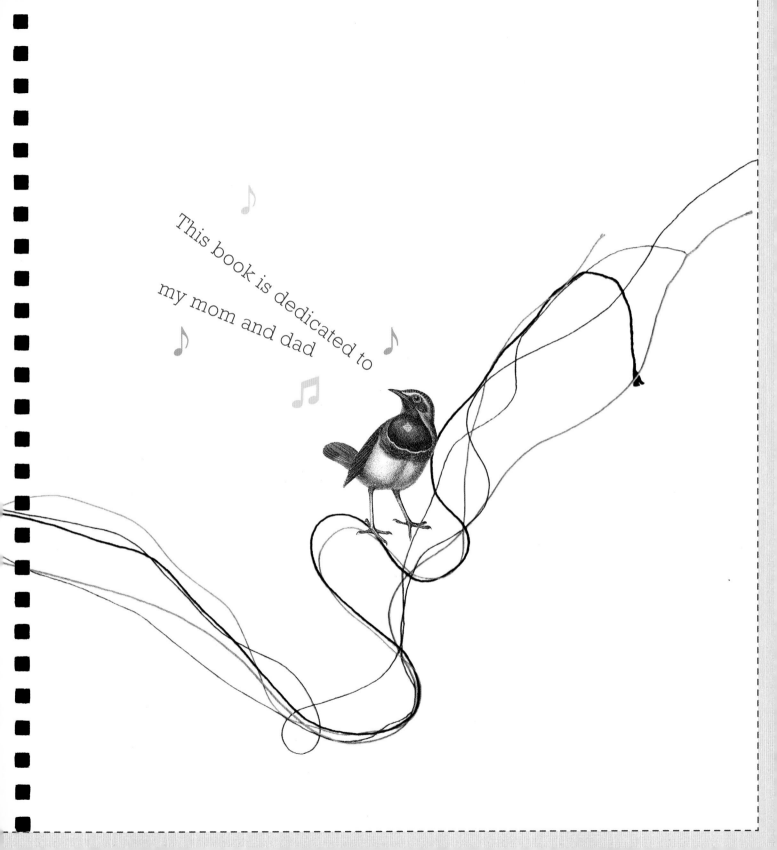

This book is dedicated to my mom and dad

Contents

INTRODUCTION

My experience with sewing has been as haphazard as the rest of my past.

When I was a kid, my mom sewed, knitted, and crocheted. My brother and I would go with her to the local fabric store in Michigan, where I grew up. We didn't have a lot of money, but I've always been a clotheshorse, so staying on trend was something that I was conscious of from an early age.

My mom would try to convince us that the clothes in the pattern books were just silhouettes, and not to pay attention to the featured fabric or styling—all of that was alterable. But that was pretty hard for me to envision as a preteen, since I just wanted to dress as well as my classmates. Still, she did what she could to make things for us in order to cut corners. In the end, I ended up using my summer job money to buy things that were too extravagant for any reasonable mom on a budget to buy her label-hungry daughter. You know—Coach bags, Guess jeans, Izod tops.

Like most children of the 1980s, I learned to sew in home ec. But we made throw pillows, not clothing. This was safe territory for my teacher, and in hindsight, I don't blame her at all for steering clear of sizing and fit. My first attempt at sewing clothing was in junior high, when I convinced my mom to help me sew a floor-length white cotton A-line skirt. Why I chose this, I'm not really sure. And as expected, it quickly did not live up to my expectations and was never finished.

After that, I didn't sew again until college. I went to art school right out of high school, the first of many stops along my higher-education journey, and got a part-time job at a local fabric store. There I noticed women who were making things for their real lives. I had been getting Vogue since I was 13, but this was the first time I saw real women sewing the things I saw on those magazine pages to wear to work or out to dinner. It was inspiring.

Not long after, I bought a sewing machine. I started sewing nearly my whole wardrobe. Of course, as a beginning sewer, nothing was fitted or tailored, and I did everything I could to avoid having to insert a zipper! I've been successfully avoiding these details my whole life, and I can help guide you to do the same as you start on your own adventure.

My love of sewing continued through my twenties. Later, at the School of the Art Institute of Chicago, I had more inspiration than I could hold on to. There I met lifelong friends—the most inspiring, intelligent, and creative people I've ever met. Like me, some of these people made stuff. You know, not exactly art for museum walls, but things for real life that were hand-sewn, screenprinted, or knitted.

Eventually, one of the ladies I knew teamed up with a

Milieu du dos—Placez cette ligne sur le pli
ntro de atrás—Colóquese esta línea sobre el dobl...

friend and started the Renegade Craft Fair. There I sold my clothing alongside other friends in this newly dubbed D.I.Y. movement. This wasn't supposed to be a business. It was renegade, after all. Punk rock is implied right there in the name. But what happened next was amazing: Many of my friends, including myself, turned these hobbies into real businesses.

Since then, I have moved to Los Angeles and launched my own clothing line. Now I'm hoping to inspire each of you to join the D.I.Y. craze. I told you it was a haphazard path!

WHAT'S INSIDE?

This book is for the modern woman who wants to make her own wardrobe. You don't want homespun, and you don't want difficult—you want hip, modern, and easy.

This book will answer that call. I have designed a collection of easy-to-make garments for each and every season and situation. Everything you need is included—sundresses, cocktail dresses, tops, skirts, jackets, even lingerie. All of the projects are timeless yet hip, without zippers or buttonholes, and each can be made in less than one day.

These projects will appeal to sewers at every ability level, from absolute beginner to advanced. Who knows? You experienced seamstresses might even learn something new! And besides, no one has to know that it was easy to make.

Each project has endless variations, so not only can you make each item in its original form, but—if you remove the sleeves, add a ruffle, and change the fabric—you can also make a completely different dress. Get creative, mix it up, and make it your own. What's most exciting to me is to see how you style and change the basics I offer. So customize to your heart's content.

This book is organized with basic sewing knowledge, skills, and tools first, followed by the sewing projects, listed seasonally. Most of these garments can be worn at any time of year, but sometimes it's nice to see how they translate to a certain season or situation just by changing the fabric. Included with each project is a list of items to help you prepare before you begin sewing—a list of notions; yardages of fabric required for fabrics both 45" wide (114cm) and 60" wide (152.5cm); techniques used within the project; and a difficulty scale from 1 to 5, with 5 being the most difficult. Keep in mind that even a level 5 project is for a beginner; it's just slightly harder than, say, a level 1 project.

Ultimately, this book is meant to empower you and teach you that you, too, can be a modern day couturier—yes, you! Now go sew, and wow your family, your friends, and yourself again and again.

Let's Get Started

Aren't you excited? You're about to learn how to sew. Soon you will be able to make some of your own clothes, and after that, who knows? The possibilities are endless.

In this section you will learn all of the basics of sewing. I'll explain what tools you need, how to lay out your pattern pieces, and what these new, unfamiliar terms mean. (What the heck is a nap, you ask? Well, it doesn't involve sleeping, I'll tell you that!)

If you feel intimidated, don't. Everyone screws up when he or she is learning something new. So will you. Once you learn to accept that from the beginning, you'll be fine. And from my experience, half the flaws you see no one else even notices. So don't go pointing them out to anyone. Just wear your new items with pride. Take your time, relax, be patient, and have fun with it. Because if it isn't fun, why do it in the first place?

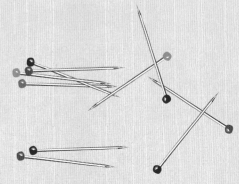

Learning the Basics

SEWING AREA

Let's face it: A lot of us don't have a guestroom to dedicate to sewing. Sure, some of you might, but many do not. Fear not—you really do not need much space. I promise that even if you live in a studio apartment, you can do this.

Here's what you need:

A table and a chair: The table can be a basic folding card table that you can store under your bed, or it can be your kitchen table, dining table, or desk. Essentially, you need something sturdy enough to hold your sewing machine. It doesn't have to be anything fancy. Any chair will do, but the more comfortable, the better.

Good light: If you have access to natural light, that's the best place to park your worktable. If you need more light, a good clip light attached to your table will do wonders. You will be working with needles and thread, and the last thing you want to do is stick yourself with a pin.

A place to cut: You can use the same table you're using for sewing, or you can use the floor. You'd be surprised to know just how many good sewers use their floors; you're not alone.

ORGANIZATION AND STORAGE

You don't need a lot of tools to get the basics done, but once you get involved in this new hobby, you might start collecting more than you thought you might. So keeping all your bits and pieces organized will keep frustration at bay when you are trying to find a tool you need to finish a dress you are working on.

HERE ARE SOME POINTERS:

If your bed has some room under it, under-the-bed bins are great places to store your equipment. These bins keep fabric out of sight and away from pet hair and dust. If there's no room under your bed, use plastic bins that fit in your closet. Another great way to store fabric in your closet is to hang it as you do your clothes; if you have room, invest in some pant and skirt hangers with clips. This will help keep your fabric wrinkle-free. Other inexpensive closet organizers—such as over-the-door shoe hangers, wall hooks, and storage systems meant for jewelry—are great for storing tools.

If you have a wall to dedicate to your tools, pegboards and corkboards are chic, inexpensive ways to get organized fast. Another good place to store tools is in a hardware toolbox. These are inexpensive and available at nearly every hardware store. For a more stylish version, use a great looking tote bag with pockets and zippers. If you have a desk to use for storage, desk organizers for the drawers are another great place to store all the little tools you gather along the way. And never underestimate just how handy Ziploc™ bags can be.

ESSENTIAL TOOLS

Investing in good tools will save you a lot of headaches down the road. You don't need to buy the world's most expensive scissors, but getting a good pair that are meant for fabric will make your cuts cleaner and keep your fabric from looking as if you had chewed it from the bolt.

HERE ARE ALL THE BASICS (PLUS A FEW SPLURGES!):

Bent-Handled Scissors

Bent-handled scissors are step 1, along with a sewing machine. You really cannot sew without them. Opting for a cheap orange-handled pair is fine, but I can't emphasize enough what a good pair of all-metal bent-handled sharp scissors will do for you. And the bent handle is important. It allows you to place the lower blade flat on the cutting surface for a more precise cut. These scissors will save you a ton of time, enabling you to cut quickly and cleanly. This is one of the few items you should splurge on. And once you buy a good pair, you can just sharpen them over and over again, which will actually save you money in the long run.

Pinking Shears

Have you seen garments with adorable zigzag edges and wondered to yourself, "How'd they do that?" This is how. Pinking shears look just like regular scissors, but if you open them up, you'll see that there are pointy triangular teeth where the blades are. These scissors are great for decoration, but they are also very practical, as you can finish off a seam just by snipping it with this handy tool. Believe it or not, fabric won't fray when cut this way. But always test it on a scrap first, because some silks and satins do not like being cut by these shears.

Rotary Cutter

This is not a necessity, but if you find that you are doing a lot of sewing, this is a smooth and fast way to cut. It is pretty much all I use to cut. It's like a round razor blade, or a pizza cutter, and is great for curves. But don't forget to be wary of what's under the fabric. I have a cheap plastic folding table from an office supply store that I cut on because I don't want to mark up my hardwood floors or my dining table. You can also get a cutting mat to protect your surface.

13

Cutting Mat

A good cutting mat can go a long way. If you need to cut a buttonhole, or if you're going to use a rotary cutter, a cutting mat can protect whatever surface is underneath. These mats range from tiny to gigantic. What you're going to use it for dictates the size you should buy. For most basic needs, a mat that is 8½" x 11" (21.5cm x 28cm) or 16" x 20" (40.5cm x 51cm) will do just fine.

Tape Measure

There are a variety of ways you can measure what you need for sewing. The easiest way is to use flexible tape measures. They usually come in smooth plastic or cloth, are 60" (152.5) long, and can bend and move with whatever you're lining them up against. And you can drape it over your neck and look all professional.

Ruler

Another good measuring tool is a basic ruler. You can use just about any ruler, but the transparent ones make it a whole lot easier to see what's underneath. Rulers are useful when you need to cut a straight edge with a blade or rotary cutter.

Pins

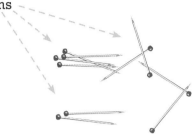

If you go to a fabric store, you might be overwhelmed by the variety of pins available. Each has a name that designates its intended use. But let's face it: Basically, a pin is a pin. Everyone has a preference, and you will, too, once you get going. There are some with round ball heads, some with flat heads, and some that are longer than others. Just be careful when pinning fabric that is not self-repairing. Always test on a scrap first to see whether the hole goes away when you pull the pin out.

Hand-Sewing Needles

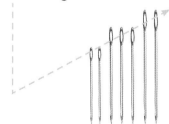

As with pins, there are lots of different kinds of needles available. I'm sure I'll get chastised for this, but I have never paid attention to what the needles were meant for. I just use whatever I have on hand. You will need them for closing seams, attaching hooks and eyes, and for repairing garments. A basic all-purpose needle, sizes 1–12, will do just fine.

Machine Needles

Each machine comes with a basic needle. You can also get different kinds for different fabrics. Likely, you will use either a sharp needle or a ballpoint needle. A regular sharp needle, sizes 9–18, will create even stitching with most woven fabrics. A ballpoint needle, sizes 9–16, has a slightly rounded point, and is good for knit fabrics. There is also a wedge-point needle, which is good for leather and vinyl. The shape of the wedge-point needle helps the material heal itself.

Pincushion

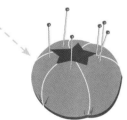

While you're sewing, you will use pins all the time. So having a quick, easy, handy, and safe place to store them is essential. Pincushions come in a variety of forms. My favorites are the basic soft fabric–covered shapes that you stick pins into and the ones that can be worn on a wristband. I have also seen lots of designers use magnetic trays meant for paper clips.

Thread

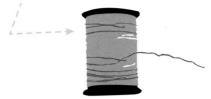

Obviously, you'll need to familiarize yourself with thread. It is the tool that links fabrics together. The thread you will use most is an all-purpose mercerized cotton-wrapped polyester. This is available in every imaginable color, but don't think that you must use thread that matches your fabric. There are metallic, variegated colors that shift from one color to another, and to everything in between. Of course, if you want to match the fabric, take a swatch of your fabric to the store and unroll a bit of thread to see how it looks on top of the fabric. If you can't find a perfect match, always go with a thread shade a bit darker than the fabric, rather than lighter.

Seam Ripper

Let's face it, everyone needs a seam ripper. I have three. Sure, you might think that you will sew each and every seam perfectly the first time out, but no, you won't. I've been sewing for years, and I still use mine all the time. These are cheap and easy to get at any sewing supply store. Using the point to pull out the seams is not only fast, but also a lot safer than using scissors—both for you and for your garment.

15

Pointer

You might think that this tool is a frill, but trust me, you will want one. Turning tie belts right side out will be made a whole lot easier when you can slip this guy into the corners of the belt and instantly get a clean, crisp point.

Weights

Using weights to hold down your pattern and fabric can make cutting go a lot faster. But here's a perfect example where you really don't need to go buy something that the pros use. There are many options for weights right there in your home. Personally, I'd use canned goods. They are cheap, they're easy to find, and they won't mar your fabric. And when you're done cutting, you can have a delicious bowl of soup.

Tailor's Chalk

When marking on fabric, you must be super careful. You don't want to use something that will show on your finished garment, but you will need to make marks on your fabric from time to time. No matter what you use, mark lightly and on the inside of your garment if possible. Tailor's chalk will brush off, but tailor's wax will not. So be sure you know what you have bought before you make any marks.

Chalk Pencil

A chalk pencil is basically the same as tailor's chalk but in pencil form. This is a much easier way to mark fine lines and details. As with the tailor's chalk, be sure to use chalk, not wax, and make your marks very carefully. As always, test on a scrap of fabric first.

Iron

Often the difference between a mediocre garment and a great one is whether it was pressed with an iron or not. You don't have to spend a lot of money on an iron. I recommend getting one that can steam press, since thick, stiff cottons sometimes need that extra push to get crisp. But you can pick one up at a thrift store that will be just fine. In fact, it might even be better than the plastic ones on the market today.

Ironing Board

I know that storing a full-sized ironing board isn't necessarily practical for every living space, but if you have space for it, it will keep your garments up high, off the floor, and away from dust and pet-hair tumbleweeds. But there are alternatives, like over-the-door boards or tabletop boards, that will also work.

Sleeve Board

There are a few specialty ironing tools to consider, and this is one of them. A sleeve board is like a miniature ironing board that makes ironing a sleeve a breeze, as you can slip the board into the sleeve of a garment and thus prevent creasing.

Tailor's Ham

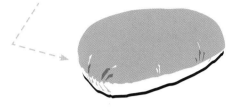

Another specialty ironing tool is a tailor's ham. It is shaped almost like a football and allows you to place a curve on the curve of the ham and iron flat. Have you ever tried to iron something like a hat on a flat board? This makes ironing those shapes easy.

17

SEWING MACHINE

Obviously, if you plan to make any of these projects, you will need a sewing machine. The variance in what you might buy is huge. There are inexpensive plastic versions, expensive machines with computers, and vintage metal workhorses. As long as you can make a straight stitch and a zigzag, you are pretty much all set.

ANATOMY OF A MACHINE

Each sewing machine will have its own quirks, and your owner's manual will be a priceless resource. If you've bought a used machine and didn't get a manual, look up the brand online and see whether you can get a copy of one. I bought a used Singer years ago without a manual, called Singer's toll-free number, and had a photocopy of the original manual mailed to me. So give it a try.

That being said, each machine will have the basics, which I've broken down for you:

PEDAL: The speed of the machine is controlled by the foot pedal.

SLIDE PLATE: This plate slides open to reveal the bobbin.

BOBBIN: One of the two threads when making a stitch is stored in the bobbin, which is located under the needle and throat plates. Bobbins are either built-in or removable. Most built-in and all removable bobbin cases have an adjustable tension screw. Using a

screwdriver, turn the screw clockwise to increase tension and counterclockwise to decrease tension.

FEED: These little metal teeth are what pull the fabric through so that it can be stitched.

THROAT PLATE: The throat plate stays in place while the needle penetrates through a hole to pick up the bobbin thread underneath.

PRESSER FOOT: This foot, which is interchangeable with other specialty feet, holds the fabric in place.

FOOT PRESSURE DIAL: Correct pressure results in even feeding of the fabric. Some machines automatically adjust tension and pressure to the fabric. Always check tension and pressure on a scrap of fabric before starting to sew. Generally, the lighter the weight of the fabric, the lighter the pressure needed.

STITCH TENSION DIAL: The stitch tension dial sets the amount of pressure put on the threads while sewing. Too much pressure will result in too little thread being fed into the stitch and will cause the fabric to pucker. Too little pressure will result in a loose stitch.

BOBBIN WINDER THREAD GUIDE: On a machine with an external bobbin winder, the thread loops through this guide between the spool and winder.

STITCH SELECTION DIAL: This is where you choose between the many different stitches: zigzag, straight, and other decorative stitches.

NEEDLE POSITION: When sewing a zipper or using a specialty stitch, you might need to move the needle from the center position to a left or right position.

SPOOL PIN: Your spool of thread sits on the spool pin. Some machines have more than one spool for decorative stitching. The thread goes onto thread guides and onto the needle.

BOBBIN WINDER: The empty bobbin sits on this winder

to be threaded. When winding bobbins, always start with an empty bobbin so the thread will wind evenly.

FLY WHEEL: This wheel spins as you push down the pedal. Most machines disengage this wheel when winding bobbins.

STITCH LENGTH DIAL: The stitch length dial is on an inch scale from 0 to 20, a metric scale from 0 to 4, or a numerical scale from 0 to 9. Most regular stitching uses 10 to 15 stitches per inch.

STITCH WIDTH DIAL: When using decorative stitches and zigzag stitching, this dial can determine the width of the stitch.

REVERSE STITCH BUTTON: This button will allow you to stitch backward, and is most often used when backstitching at the start and at the end of a seam.

BUYING TIPS

Essentially all machines do the same thing. Some are a whole lot fancier than others, and if you have the money, investing in a good machine will save you a lot of trouble. But it is not absolutely necessary. What I do recommend however, is picking a good brand. Certain companies have been around for a long time. And they have been around for a reason—they're good.

I don't want to play favorites, but brands that I feel comfortable recommending are Singer, Brother, Bernina, Pfaff, and Husqvarna Viking. These companies are all good machine manufacturers. Some of these machines contain computers, and this is both a pro and a con. Sure, they can make fancy stitches, but they are more likely to break than those without computers, and they are a lot more expensive to fix. There's a reason those big metal Singers from 100 years ago still work—they are basic.

If you think you will really use the fancy bells and whistles, consider getting one of the premium models. If not, cruise your local thrift store, the Internet, yard sales, local schools looking to clean house, and friends and family members who have one stashed in an attic somewhere. Also, a lot of sewing machine repair shops sell great used machines.

TAKING YOUR MEASUREMENTS

In order for the patterns to fit your body, you should measure yourself. Trust me—it will save you a lot of grief later on if you do this first. Also, your top half and your bottom half may fit into different size groups. If this is the case, always make your dress pattern to fit the larger of the two. For example, if you have a wider bust than hips, make the garment to fit your bust. You can always take in the part that is too big.

HOW TO MEASURE YOUR BODY

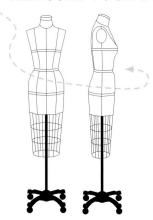

To get the most accurate measurements, it is best to measure yourself in undergarments only. If you haven't already bought yourself a measuring tape, you can use a piece of string or ribbon and lay it along side a ruler. When measuring lengths, be careful not to bend over to see the number, as this will cause the tape to bend with you. Be sure to stand up straight—no slouching—to get the most accurate measurement you can.

To measure your bust, place the tape under your arms around the fullest part of your chest, including your shoulder blades. Be sure to keep the tape measure level across your back.

When measuring your hips, keep the tape at the fullest part of your body at the top of your legs. Measure your waist at your natural waistline, just above your navel.

SIZE CHART

The patterns for the projects in this book are sized for the following measurements:

	SMALL (2–4)	MEDIUM (6–8)	LARGE (10–12)
BUST	32"–33" (81cm–84cm)	34"–35" (86cm–89cm)	36"–37" (91cm–94cm)
WAIST	24"–25" (61cm–63.5cm)	26"–27" (66cm–68.5cm)	28"–29" (71cm–74cm)
HIP	34"–35" (86cm–89cm)	36"–37" (91cm–94cm)	38"–39" (96.5cm–99cm)

SIZING FOR COMMERCIAL PATTERNS

Once you feel comfortable, go to your local fabric store and buy a commercial sewing pattern. Keep in mind that sizing for patterns can range dramatically from brand to brand, and sometimes has no relationship at all with sizing on commercially available clothing. For example, you might be a size 8 in most of the clothing you buy, but unless you know your measurements, you might go and buy a pattern for a size 8, only to realize that the measurements that

particular manufacturer designed for a size 8 are nothing like yours. So always read the sizing chart on a pattern before you buy it. Look on the back of the pattern envelope. And if you can't find it there, open the pattern (they aren't sealed) and pull out the instructional pages to find the measurement section.

USING THE PATTERNS

The projects in this book are all about mixing and matching. Almost every pattern piece is used in more than one garment. So when you cut one out and use it to make a project, be sure to keep it intact, or you might not be able to use that piece on another project.

When choosing to sew an item in this book, look at the list of pattern pieces on the first page of each project. Find the corresponding pieces on the tissue paper patterns, cut them out, and move on to the next step in the instructions.

PATTERN MARKINGS

Reading your first pattern might feel like reading a foreign language. But don't fret; it is easy as pie. Here's what to look for.

Identification Markings

Each pattern piece is marked with a number, the name of the pattern piece, and the quantity to cut. Look for the number that corresponds to your project.

Length Line

Some of the pieces are used in different lengths. For example, the Wrap Top uses the same piece as the Wrap Dress. To make the top, you cut at the longer mark and hem there. For the dress, you cut at the

Cutting Line

Notches

Pattern Number

Pattern Name

18
chic & simple
SEWING

Bodice Front
Cut 2 pieces

Quantity to Cut

Place on Fold
Bracket

Place on Grain

11
chic & simple
SEWING

Bodice Back
Cut 2 pieces

Place on Fold

Place on Grain

Cut at this length for
Wrap Dress

Dots

Cut at this length for
Wrap Top

Length Line

S
M
L

L M S

Grain Line Marking

21

shorter mark, and add a skirt to the bodice. These are all marked, so pay attention as you're cutting. If you need to cut to a shorter length, you can cut through the pattern, save the part you cut off, and tape them back together after you're done. Or you can fold the pattern up to avoid cutting it in the first place.

Grain Line Markings

Each pattern has a direction, which is called the grain. There is a grain arrow on the pattern that tells you which way the pattern piece should be placed on the fabric. The grain line should always follow the selvage of the fabric. The selvage is the finished side edge of the fabric, as opposed to the end that you have cut at the fabric store. The bias is the imaginary 45-degree angle across the fabric. This is where the fabric will stretch the most. Following these instructions is imperative. Your garment will not sew together correctly or look good on your body if the grain of the fabric is going the wrong way.

Cutting Lines

The cutting line is the outside pattern line. Each of the three sizes has been given a different line—solid for small, short dashes for medium, and long dashes for large. So when you are cutting your size, be sure to follow your line. Sometimes they overlap; just do your best to keep track of your line style.

Place on the Fold

Many of the pattern pieces are designed on the fold, which means that they show only the left- or right-hand side of a garment, and the other side is a mirror image. When this is indicated on a pattern piece, place the side of the piece with the fold line along the fold of your fabric, and cut out both sides at once. If the pattern piece does not indicate to cut on the fold, you need to cut out mirror images of each piece, one with the right side of the pattern piece facing the fabric, and vice versa. Or, cut two at once by folding the fabric in half first. For more on how to fold your fabric, read the Folding the Fabric section on page 23.

CONSTRUCTION MARKINGS

In addition to cutting instructions, some patterns contain sewing instructions. It is best to keep your pattern piece nearby when sewing because you will need to refer to these markings.

Dots

Circle dots have a few uses, indicating places to gather or indicating sections of the seam to leave open—the project instructions will tell you which. When making your project, mark the dots on the wrong side of your fabric and use them as a guide.

Notches

Notches are triangular points that need to be lined up with a mate on another piece. Line up the two notches when pinning a seam, carefully following the instructions on the project, and your pieces will sew together correctly.

Gathering

Some pieces have a specific area in which to gather. This is marked with dots, indicating that you gather between the two dots on the fabric when constructing the garment.

CUTTING
HOW MUCH FABRIC TO BUY

Most fabrics come in one of two widths—45" or 60" (114cm or 152.5cm). Each project has a suggested amount of fabric to buy for each of these widths. However, I suggest buying extra. When you are first learning, just accept the fact that you will screw up. And that's okay. But it will be a lot less tragic if you plan ahead and get at least 1 yard (91cm) or so extra.

Also, I offer yardage suggestions as if you were creating the entire garment in one fabric, but you might choose to make the top half in a different fabric from the one you use for the bottom half. If you decide to do this, I recommend cutting out your pattern pieces and measuring how much you will need for each section.

SUGGESTED FABRICS

In the introduction to each project I disclose what fabric I chose and why. I also suggest what fabrics are best to use. It is important to follow these guidelines, or else your garment will not turn out well. For example, I would not recommend choosing a stiff, thick fabric for a dress that needs to hang and flow.

The patterns in this book are geared for woven fabrics, not for knits. Knits are stretch fabrics, like jersey and T-shirt material. No beginning sewer should venture into knits. So steer clear of those for the time being.

PREPARING FABRIC FOR CUTTING

Once you've bought your fabric and brought it home, I recommend preshrinking it by washing it the same way you would the finished garment. If you are not sure whether your fabric is washable, ask the clerks at the fabric store when you buy it.

MAKING FABRIC THREAD PERFECT

Now that you have your fabric ready to go, before you fold and cut it, you need to try to get it square. If there is a center fold that was pressed crisp when you bought it, don't assume that it will be square with the edges. There are two easy ways to make your fabric square. But do these only if you cannot get your fabric to lay square right off the bat.

Tearing the fabric is actually a good way to square up the edges. It feels a bit naughty, and the first time you do it, you'll be convinced that you're doing it wrong. But really, if you clip a small cut with your scissors at one selvage and then tear it, it will tear along a single thread, which is square with the edge. Do this only with woven fabrics, and, as always, try it on a scrap first.

Another way to square your fabric is to find and draw a thread out of the weave. This is a lot easier with a loosely woven fabric. Snip into the selvage, grab a few threads, and pull them out of the fabric.

Then, cut along the line where the threads were removed.

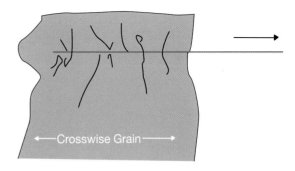

Crosswise Grain

FOLDING THE FABRIC

For the projects in this book, it is best to fold the fabric in half lengthwise, lining up the two selvage edges together. Sometimes commercial patterns will suggest a different layout, and you can follow those under those circumstances. But for these projects, this is really an easy and universal way to go.

Fold your fabric in half, selvage to selvage, and smooth it flat. If you line up your cut edges and the fabric doesn't lay flat, shift the cut ends, keeping the selvages lined up, until the fabric is square. Silk and satin fabrics can be slippery, so when cutting those, pin or place weights along the selvage to keep the fabric in place. Again, if your fabric isn't cut correctly on the grain, it will not sew or fit right, so this is important.

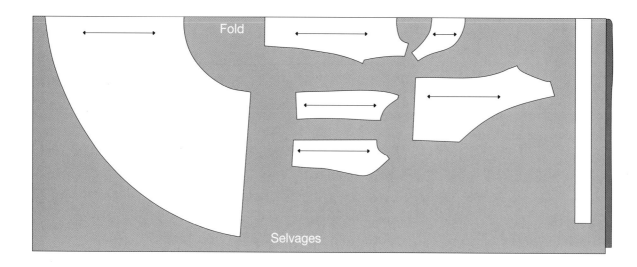

Fold

Selvages

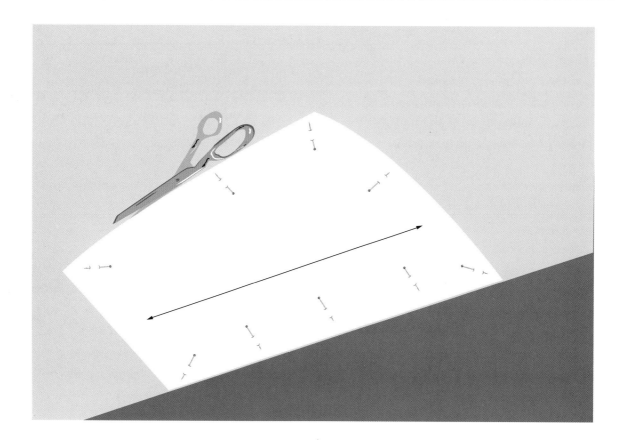

CUTTING LAYOUT

Once you've decided which project to make, cut your pattern pieces, and chosen your fabric, you will need to put the pattern pieces and the fabric together. Each pattern piece will tell you how many you need to cut. Sometimes you will need to cut more than one. In that case, you will need to cut one, move the pattern, and cut another. Always follow the grain lines and watch for the place-on-fold markings.

I do not give a suggested layout for each project's pattern pieces; however, if you buy fabric based on my suggested amounts, I am assuming that you are going to do your best to make the most of that fabric and waste as little as possible. Items that don't need to be placed on the fold can use the rest of the fabric. Or to use a piece meant for the fold elsewhere, you can lay the mirror piece down, cut half, flip the pattern piece over, being careful to keep it lined up with your first cut, and cut the other half.

HOW TO CUT

Cutting seems self-explanatory, right? Well, maybe, but I do have a few pointers:

First, I cannot emphasize enough the importance of good bent-handled scissors. The bend in the handle allows for the bottom blade to cleanly glide along your cutting surface.

Second, making long, smooth motions with your cutting will make cleaner lines than making short, quick, and jagged cuts. Placing your hand on your fabric to support and hold it down is also helpful, even if your item is pinned and/or weighed down. Cut carefully around corners and curves, and always include any notches.

ONE-WAY FABRICS

Some fabrics are one-way fabrics, which means there is one way in which they should be worn. When cutting this kind of fabric, cut the pieces out in the correct direction so you can wear the fabric in the right way.

Corduroy and velvet are two common one-way fabrics. They have a nap to the fabric, which is smooth when you rub your hand in one direction, and rough in the opposite direction. Short nap fabrics like these should be cut with the nap (the smooth direction) running toward the top. So if you run your hands up the nap of a pair of corduroy pants, it will be smooth. This will give you the richest color. Long nap fabrics, like fleece and velour, should be cut with the nap running towards the hem.

ONE-WAY PRINTS

Certain prints also have a direction to them. For example, let's say you went to a thrift store and scored some great vintage fabric with cute puppies on it. But the puppies are only upright when holding the fabric in one direction. This is a one-way print. When you cut a fabric like this, you will want to be sure that you're not turning the print upside down on your skirt. Other one-way prints, which might not seem like prints at all, are certain shiny fabrics. Sometimes the shine is directional.

One-way prints are best cut with the right side up. This way you can see exactly what you're cutting when you're doing it.

25

Finding Your Style

I know you don't need me to tell you about your own personal style. But if you bear with me, I do have some pointers on some zippy additions that can help customize your new handmade wardrobe. Following some of these tips can also make one project look like ten different ones, as each variation can be trimmed in a unique and fun way.

FABRIC

I have a problem with fabric. There, I admitted it. Hi, my name is Christine, and I'm a fabric addict. I'm sorry to say that this might happen to you too. Sure, while you wander your local fabric store, or worse, the Internet at 2 a.m., you'll convince yourself that you'll use it for "something." You might. But don't let the fabric store overwhelm you. Here's my best advice: Go in with a plan. Leave yourself open to inspiration—you don't want to be too rigid—but have some idea of what you want: floral print, silk, corduroy. Otherwise, you might find yourself with a whole lot of fabric but none that works with the party dress pattern you had intended to shop for.

FABRIC TYPES

The patterns in this book are intended for woven fabrics. What are woven fabrics? They have threads that are actually woven together, like a basket weave, for example. You've seen baskets that are woven together with stiff straw or twigs, right? Well, it's like that, but with thread.

Conversely, knit fabrics are knitted together. Seems obvious right? It is that simple. Just like a scarf that a family member knitted for you, knit fabric threads are looped in the same way. That is what makes them stretch, much like your scarf. Knits are quite hard for a beginner sewer, and require different stitching in order for the stretch to work. So just stick to woven fabrics for the projects in this book, and you'll be all set.

DIRECTIONAL PATTERNS

As I mentioned on page 25, some patterns are intended to go only one way. But that's not the only directional pattern to consider using. Another great one that instantly creates a custom look is a border print, which is a fabric that has an edge with a border on it. This allows you to cut your pattern out of the area of the fabric without the border, and then cut the skirt or bottom ruffle using this border print along the bottom.

Other fabrics with directional patterns are lace and eyelet. You probably know what lace is, and if you add a lace ruffle to the bottom of a skirt, there's no need to hem it, since the beautiful scalloped lace edge will create the hem for you. Same with eyelet. See the Sunday Dress on page 49 for a gorgeous eyelet ruffled hem.

And of course, there are always stripes and plaids. Stripes tend to elongate the wearer, so there's quite a big difference between wearing stripes vertically and wearing them horizontally. Keep that in mind when you lay everything out to be cut.

DIRECTIONAL FABRICS

Similar to directional patterns are directional fabrics. Again, I briefly mentioned this on page 25, but it bears repeating here. Fabrics like moiré, corduroy, and velvet all have a direction, which needs to be considered when laying out your pattern pieces.

COLOR, PRINTS, AND TEXTURES

When thinking of how to approach your garments, feel free to consider doing it the way I have. But stretch your imagination, and it can be even better, as well as more uniquely *you*. Choose something that expresses your own personality.

COLOR

I love seeing a crisp dress with contrasting trim. Really think about all the different pieces of the puzzle and how you can change them up. You can make a plain black dress, but if you punch it with a red ruffle at the bottom, it becomes something else altogether.

PRINTS

What is true with color is also true with prints. Now, I'm not one who sticks to the rules when it comes to fashion. Haven't you seen those women wearing a floral dress with polka dot trim and wonder how they do it? One good rule to mixing prints that are not supposed to go together is to stick to a rigid color scheme. For example, choose a pink, orange, and black floral print, and mix it with a white with black polka dot trim. Another good rule is to pick one dominant print and one much smaller accent print.

TEXTURES

So now that I've taught you how to use a napped fabric like corduroy, here I'm going to tell you to forget all about that! But seriously, I once saw a pair of corduroy pants with the wale going horizontally around the legs, and I thought it was so unique. I really believe that there are no rules here, so knock yourself out.

NOTIONS AND FINISHING DETAILS

The difference between a good garment and a great one is often found in the finishing details. Just about anyone can make a cute black dress, but top it off with an amazing handmade belt, or topstitch it with metallic silver thread, and it is way more than just an LBD (a. k. a., little black dress).

DECORATIVE TRIMS

There are so many decorative trims that I couldn't even begin to cover them all here. That's a whole other book. But some deserve special mention, like rickrack. Rickrack gets a bit of a bad rap sometimes. It's often considered too crafty or too little girlish. But I beg to differ. Rickrack can add instant vintage flair to a hem. Here's how:

To add rickrack to the right side of your hem, and show the whole trim, just make your hem as normal, then sew the rickrack with a straight stitch directly to the front. You can either have the entire trim up on the fabric, or have it so that only half is on the fabric, with the other half below the hem, lending the rickrack's wavy edge to the hem itself.

Or you can do the opposite and add rickrack to the wrong side of your finished hem. Then, you see just half the zigzag peeking out from under your skirt. I once made a black A-line skirt and added large white rickrack to the inside of the skirt—everyone loved it. It was sweet and vintagey, but also a little punk rock.

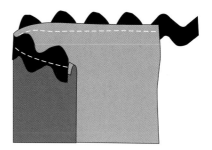

DECORATIVE THREAD

Another great and easy embellishment is using a contrasting thread on your hem or when you are topstitching. I mean, you have to stitch the hem anyway, so how much more work is it to change the thread to something different? However, keep in mind that if you're doing this, you are going out of your way to point it out, so you had better sew it particularly well. If you have a black skirt, and you add white stitching to it, trust me, everyone will notice. So take your time and do it right. And if you don't, that's exactly what the seam ripper is for.

ELASTIC

Okay, so elastic isn't exactly a decorative detail, but once it is encased inside your sleeve it is. Many of the projects included with sleeves are finished off with elastic. It adds a special touch to an otherwise simple beginner garment. And it really hides a lot. If you screw up the elastic cuff hem, no one will notice. But if you mess up a real hem, that will likely be seen. The gathering that elastic provides for you can hide many flaws.

BUTTONS

None of the projects in this book have buttonholes. But the cape does have buttons. There's no reason why you can't sew buttons in places where they aren't functional. Take, for example, the Baby Doll Dress on page 87. You can absolutely add buttons to the front of the bodice in a vertical line down the center, just before the gathering. Or on the Sundress on page 62, where the straps meet the top casing, instead of sewing the straps into the casing, you could finish the ends off and attach them to the casing with adorable buttons. You really don't need a buttonhole or a functional use to add buttons at all!

HOOKS AND EYES

Used more for actually closing an opening in a garment than for decoration, hooks and eyes are the underappreciated closure of the sewing family. These days, they are used most often to top zippers off. But years ago, this was the button alternative. For the back of the Baby Doll Top on page 46 and the Baby Doll Dress on page 87, I suggest using hooks and eyes to close the neckline in lieu of a buttonhole and button. They achieve the same end but are much easier to use for a beginner.

BIAS TAPE

On page 39 I have a whole section on how to make your own bias tape and sew it onto your garment. But here, let's talk about its decorative capabilities. Really, they are endless. Especially since you will soon know how to make your own. So you can make the Jacket on page 98 in rich white wool, and trim the edges off in red plaid. It can instantly provide a custom look. And you can add it in places not called for in the projects, like on hems.

BELTS

A chic belt can really make an outfit. And for a beginning sewer, I have designed many of the waists of the projects to be finished with elastic, which is fine. But sometimes you'll want something cleaner and more stylish. Here are a variety of belts to try:

TIE BELT

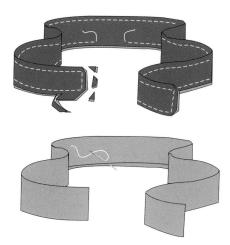

The most repeated belt in the projects is the tie belt. It is basically a long strip of fabric that you tie around your waist—easy, customizable, and totally effective.

1. Cut out pattern piece 01-A for the tie belt. Lay it on the fold of the fabric you want to use, and cut out the number of pieces called for in the project instructions. With right sides facing, stitch around both short ends and one long edge. Stitch the other long edge, leaving an opening about 2" (5cm) wide. Clip the corners of the seams to reduce bulk.

2. Turn the tie right side out through the opening, and press crisp. Fold the seam allowance into the opening, press, and slipstitch closed.

RIBBON BELT

A ribbon belt couldn't be easier. Seriously, there's not even any sewing involved, just scissors.

1. Find a decorative ribbon. Keep in mind that when tied, both sides will show, so if you choose velvet, look at the back side to see whether it is pretty enough to be shown or not. Fold the ribbon in half lengthwise.

2. Using your scissors, snip the end of the ribbon at an angle and unfold to find a finished-looking end.

BUCKLE WITHOUT A PRONG

Some buckles have prongs, and some do not. If you find you are in love with a buckle with a prong, just remove the prong and follow these instructions to make a belt with the buckle.

1. Find a buckle that you love. Follow the directions for the tie belt and make it about ½" (13mm) narrower than your buckle's center post width.
2. Wrap one end of the tie around the center post of the buckle and stitch the end to the back of the tie by hand.

GATHERED BELT

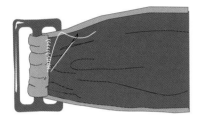

With a gathered belt, you deliberately choose too much fabric for the width of your buckle so that it gathers at the buckle.

1. Find a buckle to match your garment. Follow the directions for the tie belt, except make this tie about double the width of the buckle post.
2. Wrap one end around the buckle post, forcing all the fabric to gather inside the width of the buckle. Hand stitch the end of the tie to the back of the tie.

FABRIC BELT CARRIERS

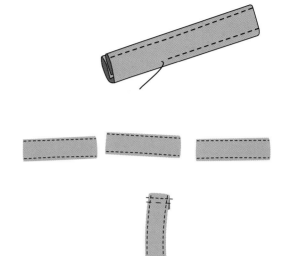

You might decide that you want to have loops on your garment to keep the belt in place. This would look really snappy on the Trench on page 57, and you can even tie the belt back behind your waist, looped through the side belt carriers—so chic.

1. Use pattern piece 03 for making bias tape. Lay that on the fabric of your choice and cut out. Fold the strip in half lengthwise, wrong sides together, and press. Open the center fold, fold each half in to meet the center fold, and press again. Close the strip at the center fold and stitch close to the edge on both long sides.
2. Measure the width of your belt, add 1" (2.5cm), and cut the desired number of strips at this length.
3. Fold down each end of each strip ¼" (6mm) and press. Pin in place on your garment and try it on with the belt to make sure the placement is correct. Using a straight stitch, sew two rows each along the top and bottom of the strips to secure them to the garment.

31

Basic Techniques

In order to sew clothing, there are a few techniques you need to learn. Everything from how to sew a basic seam to how to attach a bodice to a skirt with inserted elastic is included here, though I have omitted techniques that are beyond the scope of the projects, like how to insert a zipper. Each project has a list of techniques used, so you can read up on that topic before you start if you are not sure how to do it.

BASIC STITCHING

Okay, so maybe you are an absolute sewing newbie. That's okay! What's important is that you're starting now. Don't be afraid; I will teach you all the basics to get you started.

STITCHING A SEAM FROM START TO FINISH

When people refer to a seam, they are talking about the place where thread joins two pieces (or more) of fabric together. Look at what you're wearing. Where the front and the back of your top, dress, pants, or skirt come together, there is likely a seam.

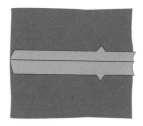

1. Most often you will place the right sides of your chosen fabric facing together, with the edges of the pieces aligned with each other. The right side is the side that is worn on the outside—the side that you want people to see. Using pins, attach the fabric together, making sure that you pull the pins out when stitching before they go under the machine needle. You will break needle after needle if you don't.

2. Starting at one end of the seam, stitch about ½" (13mm) and stop. Pushing your backstitching button on your machine, backtrack over the stitches you have just made, sewing in the reverse direction. This is called backstitching. Sew back to the beginning of your seam. Then, release the backstitching button and sew forward along the rest of your seam until you get to the end. Before the

needle runs off the fabric, sew another backstitch. This prevents the thread from pulling out and locks it into place.

3. Using an iron that is set to the temperature for your fabric choice, press open your seam from the inside of the garment. Turn the garment over and press the seam on the right side to get it nice and crisp.

SEAM ALLOWANCE

When you stitch a seam, you stitch inside the edge of the fabric, a measured distance from that edge. The fabric between your stitching and the edge is the seam allowance. The projects in this book call for a ⅝" (16mm) seam allowance. This is what most commercial patterns use as well. The throat plate on your machine has guideline measurements on it, and there will be one for this distance. This seems like a small thing, but if you are too close to or too far from the edge, the seams won't line up, and the fit will not be right. So be sure to stitch as close to the seam allowance as possible.

GUIDING FABRIC

When you are sewing for the first time, sometimes it is tricky to get comfortable. Where do I put my hands? Do I push the fabric through, or do I pull it out the other side of the needle? You will get the hang of it, and there is no right or wrong way to place your hands to get comfortable. However, you do want to treat the fabric right as as the needle passes through it. The best approach is to guide the fabric. To guide it is to do exactly what that sounds like—to support it, direct it, steer it. Don't push it, and don't pull it. Just help it along its journey under the needle.

STITCHING CURVES

A lot of patterns have curved edges to them. Arm holes, neck holes, and bust seams will likely be curved. These can be tricky to sew, but with some practice, you will get it in no time.

Guide your curve while paying close attention to your seam allowance. If you at any point need to turn the fabric, lower the needle into the fabric, raise the presser foot, pivot the fabric, lower the presser foot, and continue sewing. To get an even stitch when sewing a curve, shorten your stitch length and slow down your sewing speed.

CLIPPING AND NOTCHING SEAMS

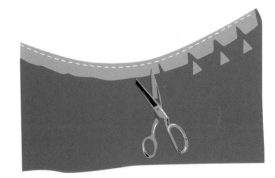

When you sew a curve, there is added bulk in the seam allowance because the inside of the curve is smaller than the outside. In order to get the seam to lie flat, you will need to clip or notch the seam. Clipping refers to slits that are cut into the seam allowance, and notches are triangular segments that are cut out of the seam allowance. Be very careful not to cut too close to the stitching on your seam, as this will make it weak.

BASTING

Sometimes you will need to hold two or more pieces of fabric together, but only temporarily. When this is required, a basting stitch is used. This stitch is just like a regular straight stitch, except it is set to be longer than a regular stitch. Also, as you will likely remove the baste stitch after you sew your seam, do not backstitch at the start or finish of the seam. Basting is also used in this book for gathering a seam.

SEAM FINISHING

Finishing a seam means to keep the seam allowance fabric from fraying and to make the inside of your garment neat and tidy. There are many ways to finish a seam; the two easiest are zigzagging and pinking. I recommend finishing your fabric edges before you begin to construct any garment, as it can be a whole lot trickier to try to do it after the fact.

To zigzag finish a seam, set your machine to a zigzag stitch with a medium length and width. Start at one end of your fabric edge, and stitch as close to the edge as you can without going over. If you have some distance between the zigzag and the edge, trim off the excess. But if you haven't sewn your seam yet, be sure to account for the width you removed, as this will affect your ⅝" (16mm) seam allowance.

To finish a seam with a pinked edge, use your pinking shears and clip the edges of your fabric. Not all fabrics can be finished in this way, so be sure to try it first on a scrap. Silks and satins, for example, typically do not like pinking shears. And as with the zigzagged finish, account for any width you've trimmed off in your seam allowance.

PRESSING

The difference between a crisp, professional garment and a marshmallowy soft one is often the difference between ironing and not ironing. Many times I have sewn something, thought it looked bad, and then pressed it crisp, only to see that it really looks good after all.

SEAMS

Iron your garment, but it is equally as important, if not more so, to iron your seams. After you stitch a seam, it is best to iron it right then and there. But when your garment is all finished, I recommend giving all the seams a crisp press. The improvement you will see in your hems will amaze you.

Here are some basic rules to follow:

1. Press every seam after you sew it, especially before you combine it with another seam.
2. Press with a soft gentle movement, using less heat to start, and then work your way up to higher temperatures.
3. Never press over pins, needles, or anything else that can either get super hot or melt.
4. Always test press a scrap of fabric first to see how it will behave.
5. Listen to your iron's suggestions of heat temperature for your desired fabric choice.

GATHERS

Pressing a gathered hem can be tricky. But like all other ironing, it is very noticeable when you don't take the time to press it crisp. And if you plan on washing your gathered garment, you'll likely have to press it again before wearing. So you might as well just accept the idea that you'll have to do this.

To press a gathered seam, point your iron towards the gathered seam. Stick the point of the iron into the gathers, not across the top of them. While you press the iron into the gather, smooth the folds underneath the iron to avoid creasing the fabric. It is easier if you start at one side seam and work your way around the item, so you know where you started.

FINISHING DETAILS

Once you've mastered the basics—buying a machine, learning how to thread it, stitching your first two pieces of fabric together—you're ready for more. These techniques will take you from sewing a seam to making something more elaborate.

PATCH POCKETS

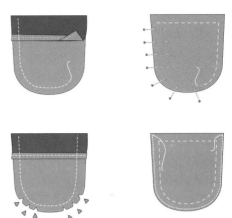

Pockets come in nearly every shape and size. The ones I have included in my projects are a basic rounded bottom patch pocket. A patch pocket is sewn directly onto the front of a garment, as opposed to a pocket that is, say, set into a side seam.

1. Find pattern piece 16 for the patch pocket and cut around the perimeter of the pattern. Lay it on your fabric, with the grain either vertically up the pocket or on the bias, and cut out the number of pockets you desire.

   Fold the top edge of the pocket down, wrong sides together, about ¼" (6mm), and press. Fold another ¼" (6mm), stitch the fold in place, and press crisp. Fold the top edge of the pocket down, right sides together, along the fold line. Stitch around the pocket ⅝" (16mm) from the edge, including the fold.

2. Turn the top of the pocket right side out. Clip the seams at the rounded corners of the pocket so that it will lay flat. You may want to use a pointer to get the corners sharp. Fold the seam allowance into the pocket, wrong sides together, and press. Be sure

35

to fold in the stitch line you have made so that it doesn't show on the front of the pocket.

3. Following the placement markings on the pattern, pin the pocket to the garment with the wrong side of the pocket against the right side of the garment. Baste the two together. With a straight stitch, sew along the side and bottom edges of the pocket, getting as close to the edge as you can without going over, to attach the pocket to the garment. Remove your basting stitches and press crisp.

CASINGS AND INSERTING ELASTIC

The most basic of casings is the fold-down casing. This is commonly used on waistbands and sleeve hems inserted with elastic. Many of the projects I've designed for this book are finished in this way. It may not be the most couture method, but it is very effective for a beginning sewer. If you don't like the way the waistband looks with elastic, you can always top it off with a belt, a vintage scarf, or a wide piece of ribbon.

1. Fold down the fabric ¼" (6mm), wrong sides together, and press. Fold again, creating a channel wider than the elastic you are going to insert: If you are using ½" (13mm) elastic, fold down 1" (2.5cm); if you are using ¼" (6mm) elastic, fold down ½" (13mm). Press flat and pin for sewing.

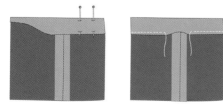

2. Starting at one of the garment's side seams, sew with a straight stitch close to the edge of the first fold, and sew around the entire casing. Stop about 1" (2.5cm) short of your starting point. Do not forget to backstitch when you start and stop your sewing.

3. To insert elastic, pin a large safety pin to one end of the elastic, and feed it through the casing. Be sure not to lose the other end, and try not to twist the elastic while feeding it through. When you've gone around the whole casing, overlap and pin the two ends of the elastic together.

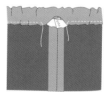

4. Using a zigzag stitch, secure the two elastic ends together. Switch back to the straight stitch and line up your needle with the stitching used to sew the casing. Close up the hole left in the garment, and remember to backstitch to secure the seam.

GATHERING

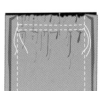

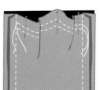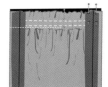

Gathering forces a larger piece of fabric into a smaller space. By pulling basted threads together, you create gathers in the fabric, making the larger piece smaller. In this book, you will see this on ruffle hems and bodice yokes. It is an easy technique that creates a nice finishing detail.

1. Using your basting stitch, sew two parallel rows within your ⅝" (16mm) seam allowance.

2. With right sides together, pin the gathered item to the item you are sewing it to, lining up the raw edges and seams.

3. Pull the two basting threads on each end while gliding the fabric along to fit into the smaller space. Evenly distribute the gathering and pin it in place.

4. Using a straight stitch, sew the two pieces together with the gathered side facing you and a ⅝" (16mm) seam allowance, just under the basting stitch. As you sew, guide the gathered fabric under the needle for even stitching, or else you will sew pleats, not gathers. Gently remove the basting stitch.

HEMS

The most basic hem is a machine-rolled hem. To make a rolled hem, on the wrong side of your fabric, fold the hem up ¼" (6mm) and press. Repeat and press again. Using a straight stitch, sew along the fold. Press crisp.

ATTACHING LACE

Adding decorative lace is a nice finishing detail, and it couldn't be easier to do. Just follow these simple steps: Using a zigzag stitch, finish the edges of your fabric so it doesn't fray. Pin the wrong side of the lace you've chosen to the right side of the fabric, so both right sides are facing you. Overlap the lace onto the fabric by about ½" (13mm). Sew where the fabric and the lace overlap, using a zigzag stitch.

SEWING ON BUTTONS

There are two main kinds of buttons—flat sew-through buttons and shank buttons. Flat sew-through buttons look exactly as they sound—they have a flat bottom and holes in the middle to sew through for attaching to fabric. Shank buttons do not have holes through them. Rather, they have a peg in the center back with a loop for stitching. Each type of button is sewn in a different way. Here's how to do it:

37

Flat Sew-Through Buttons

Mark on your garment where you want to place the button. Place the button flat and centered on that spot. Using a needle and thread, start on the inside of your garment, sew through one hole, and back down another. Do so until the button is secure, and knot off the thread on the underside.

Flat Sew-Through Buttons with Optional Shank

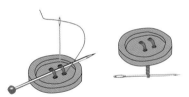

Mark on your garment where you would like to place the button. Hold the button flat and centered on that location. Using a threaded needle, start on the inside of your garment, and stitch through a hole. Before going back down another hole, place a pin, a toothpick, or a needle over the holes and loop your thread over that as you go back down to the wrong side of the garment. Repeat this until the button is secure. Remove the object you've placed on the button and raise the button and threads as high as you can. Wind the needle and thread around the threads between the button and the fabric to create a shank. Return the needle down to the wrong side of the garment and knot in place.

Shank Button

Mark on your garment where you want to sew the button. Hold the button centered on that spot. Using a needle and thread, start on the wrong side of the garment, poke through to the right side, pass the needle through the loop in the shank, and return to the wrong side. Repeat until the button is secure, return needle to the wrong side, and knot the threads in place.

Shank Button with Extended Shank

Repeat the instructions for the shank button, but raise the button with your hand to leave slack in the threads between the button and the fabric. After sewing the button on, but prior to knotting the threads, wind the needle and thread around the threads between the button and the fabric to create the extended shank. Return the needle to the wrong side and knot the threads in place.

38

MAKING HANDMADE BIAS TAPE

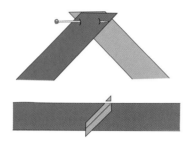

A nice and easy way to finish raw edges is to use bias tape; ½" (13mm) double-fold bias tape should be available at any fabric store, but you can also make your own. You can really zip up a garment with some contrasting tape. Think of the possibilities—vintage fabric trim, contrasting colors, or even patterned tape on a solid colored garment. The options are endless.

1. Cut out pattern piece 03 for bias tape. Lay it on your fabric, placing the grain line in the direction of the bias. Cut strips out. If you need strips longer than those which you can get in one cut, you can make more than one cut and then join them. Cut the ends at an angle.

2. With right sides together, overlap two ends at a right angle, forming a V shape. Stitch together with ¼" (6mm) seam allowance.

3. Unfold the V and press; the tape should unfold into one long, straight piece. Clip the overlapping corners.

APPLYING BIAS TAPE

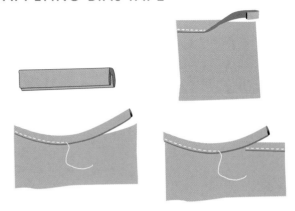

Whether you have made your own bias tape, or you have bought some from the store, you now need to know how to apply it.

1. If you have store-bought double-fold bias tape, it comes already folded. If you have made your own, you will need to press it. Fold the strip in half lengthwise, wrong sides together, and press. Open the center fold and fold each half in so that the raw edge meets the center fold. Press again.

2. To attach to a seam with raw side seams on each side, wrap the tape around the raw edge, with half the tape on one side, and half on the other, pin, and stitch in place, going through both sides of the tape and the fabric it is wrapped around.

3. When applying tape to a seam with finished side seams, wrap it around the raw edge and pin in place, leaving excess at the finished seam. At the ends, fold the tape under itself, pin, and stitch in place.

4. To finish a seam that is a circle, such as the hem of a skirt, wrap the tape around the raw edge, pin, and stitch in place. When approaching your starting point, fold the end under about ¼" (6mm), overlap the starting end, and finish with a backstitch.

39

Spring

Spring is a time of rebirth and rejuvenation. It has an implied optimism. Birds chirping, flowers blooming—spring is a time for lovers. But just as you're busting out that pink sundress, more snow comes out of nowhere. It can be a fickle season.

For this spring collection, I have designed some classic pieces with a few twists. There is a baby doll top, a classic trench coat, a cocktail dress, a sundress, a fun circle skirt, and the classic wrap dress, a must in everyone's wardrobe. These shapes will work with spring in mind, but also will work in any color, any time of year.

I like to approach spring with the idea that garments change shape, but not color . . . at least not too much, too soon. You will look really silly with a parka over a pink sundress. Once the grass in the park starts to turn green again and the birds return to the city, go for that sundress in pink with full force.

Doing It Like DVF

The Classic Wrap Dress

There's nothing more timeless than the wrap dress. Watch any makeover show, ask any stylist, cruise any department store, and they will all tell you the same thing: The wrap dress is great for every situation and for every woman. It is the most universally flattering look on all body types, and has been so for generations. Diane von Furstenberg made her first wrap dress in the 1970s and is still selling them today.

I used a sweet pink and white stretch seersucker stripe for mine. You could choose a black cotton with white screenprinted skulls and it would look just as great. Get creative and make the waist tie out of a contrasting color, or do the same with the bias tape. I chose not to add bias tape to the neckline. To get inspired by a version with bias tape, check out the Wrap Top on page 71 in the Summer chapter.

FABRIC
3¾ yd (343cm) of 45" (114cm) wide, or 3½ yd (320cm) for 60" (152.5cm) wide

NOTIONS
96" (244cm) of ½" (13mm) double-fold bias tape

¼" (6mm) elastic—Small: 12" (30.5cm); Medium: 13½" (34.5cm); Large: 15" (38cm)

SEAM ALLOWANCE
⅝" (16mm)

TECHNIQUES
Casings and inserting elastic (page 36)

Stitching curves (page 33)

Gathering (page 36)

Basting (page 34)

43

PATTERN PIECES 18 BODICE FRONT 19 BODICE FRONT SIDE 17 SLEEVE 21 BODICE BACK
20 BODICE BACK SIDE 22 SKIRT 01-A WAIST TIE (CUT TO 25" [63.5CM]) 03 BIAS TAPE (OPTIONAL)

Cut Out Your Dress

1. Cut out the pattern pieces for the dress in your size.

2. Fold the fabric crosswise instead of selvage to selvage. Lay out the pattern pieces on your dress fabric, following the grain and fold markings on the patterns. Pin them in place, and cut around the perimeter of each pattern piece. Cut two Bodice Front pieces, two Bodice Front Side pieces, two Sleeve pieces, and two Bodice Back Side pieces. Cut one Bodice Back piece, one Skirt piece, and four Waist Tie pieces on the fold of your fabric. If you choose to make bias tape, use pattern piece

03 and follow the directions in the Techniques section (page 39).

Sew Your Dress

3. With right sides together and the notches on the patterns aligned, stitch the Bodice Front and Bodice Front Side pieces together. Ⓐ Sewing this front curve can be a bit tricky, but just turn the piece along as you sew and it will be great. Sew the Bodice Back and Bodice Back Side pieces together in the same way. Ⓑ

44

4. With right sides together, stitch the Bodice Front to the Bodice Back at the shoulder seam.

5. With right sides facing, stitch the Bodice Back to the Bodice Front at the side seams, leaving an opening between the two dots marked on the pattern piece. Be sure to backstitch at the opening to secure the seam.

6. Press open the side seam with the opening. Fold the seam allowance around the opening under ¼" (6mm) and topstitch all the way around the hole to keep it open. Ⓒ

7. Fold each Sleeve piece in half crosswise, with right sides together, and stitch the short seams together. Baste around the top of the Sleeve piece, between the two dots on the top, and gather. Hold the Bodice with the wrong side out and an armhole facing you. With the right sides together, align the gathered end of one Sleeve with the armhole's raw edge, lining the seam in the Sleeve up with the side seam in the Bodice (the ungathered end of the Sleeve should be inside the Bodice); pin the Sleeve in the armhole; adjust the gathering to fit; and stitch the Sleeve to the Bodice around the armhole. Ⓓ Repeat to attach the other Sleeve to the other armhole. Turn the Bodice and the Sleeves right side out.

8. Fold the bottom of one Sleeve under about ¼" (6mm) and press. Fold under again about ½" (13mm) and press again. Stitch around the top of the fold, leaving a 1" (2.5cm) opening near the seam. Cut the elastic for your desired size. Pin a large safety pin to one end of the elastic, and feed it through the casing. Be sure not to lose the other end into the Sleeve, and try not to twist the elastic while feeding it through. When you've gone around the whole Sleeve, overlap the two ends and pin. Zigzag stitch the two elastic ends together and close up the hole left in the Sleeve with a straight stitch. Repeat for the other Sleeve.

9. Pin the Skirt piece to the Bodice, right sides together, lining up the open edges. Stitch together.

10. If you are not using bias tape, fold and press the sides of the Skirt, Bodice, and neck under ¼" (6mm). Fold under, press another ¼" (6mm), and stitch. If you are using either handmade bias tape or purchased double-fold bias tape, line up the raw end of the bias tape at the hem in the front of the dress. Starting there, pin the tape up one side of the Skirt, up the Bodice, around the neck, back down the Bodice, and down the other side of the Skirt, ending at the hem, opposite of where you started. Stitch in place.

11. With right sides together, stitch two of the Waist Tie pieces together along both long edges and one of the short ends, leaving the other short end open. Clip the corners of the seam, turn the Waist Tie right side out, and press flat. Fold the seam allowance on the raw end into the Waist Tie and press. Repeat with the remaining two Waist Tie pieces.

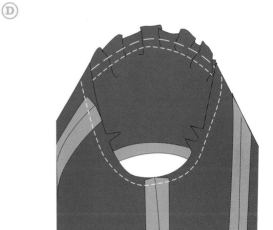

Ⓓ

12. Pin the unfinished end of the Waist Tie to the inside of the Front Bodice, just above the waist seam, between the dots on the pattern. Stitch in place. Ⓔ Repeat with the second Waist Tie and Front Bodice.

13. To finish the dress, fold up the hem—including the bias tape, if used—about ¼" (6mm) and press. Fold another ¼" (6mm), and stitch it in place around the entire Skirt.

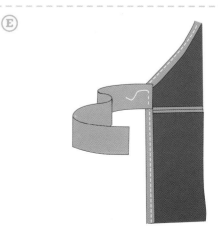

Ⓔ

45

The T-Shirt Alternative
The Baby Doll Top

If you need to run to the market or the bank, or do whatever other errands you may have, why throw on a sloppy T-shirt when you can put on something much more polished? Like its dress counterpart, this top can achieve sexy, classic, and sweet-little-girl vibes all at once.

I chose lightweight classic black-and-white polka dot stretch cotton, but pretty much any color and pattern will work with this design. I would advise you to stick to a lightweight or medium weight cotton. Just don't pick anything too stiff, or else the bottom of this top will stick out like a tent. And no one wants that.

FABRIC
2 yd (183cm) of 45" (114cm) wide, or 1¼ yd (114cm) of 60" (152.5cm) wide

NOTIONS
¼" (6mm) elastic—Small: 12" (30.5cm); Medium: 13½" (34.5cm); Large: 15" (38cm)

1 hook and eye set

SEAM ALLOWANCE
⅝" (16mm)

TECHNIQUES
Casings and inserting elastic (page 36)

Gathering (page 36)

Basting (page 34)

PATTERN PIECES 07 TOP FRONT AND BACK 04 BODICE FRONT 05 BODICE BACK 06 SLEEVE

47

Cut Out Your Top

1. Cut out the pattern pieces for the top in your size.

2. Lay the pattern pieces on your chosen fabric, aligning the indicated edge of each piece along the fold of the fabric (do not cut the Bodice Back pieces along the fold). Pin them in place, and cut around the perimeter of the pattern pieces. Cut two Top Front and Back pieces, two Bodice Front pieces, and two Sleeve pieces. Cut four Bodice Back pieces, a set of two for the right back and a mirror-image set of two for the left back.

Sew Your Top

3. With right sides together, stitch the right-hand Bodice Back piece to the right-hand shoulder of the Bodice Front. Repeat with the left-hand side, and then repeat this entire step to make a second identical set of Bodice pieces.

4. Place the two Bodice pieces right sides together, and stitch up one open center seam of the Bodice Back, around the neck, and back down the other center seam of the Bodice Back. Ⓐ Clip the seams

around the curve of the neck, turn right side out, and press flat. Pin the two sides at the base of the center of the Bodice Back to keep them together. Keep them pinned in place while you are attaching them to the Top Front and Back piece in the next step.

5. Place the right sides of the two Top Front and Back pieces together and stitch the side seams. Baste and gather the top of the two Top Front and Back pieces. Adjust the gather to fit the Bodice. Pin the Bodice in place, with right sides together and raw edges and side seams aligned. Starting at one of the side seams, stitch the Bodice to the top.

6. Fold each Sleeve piece in half crosswise, with right sides together, and stitch the short ends together. Baste around the top of each Sleeve piece, between the two dots on the top, and gather. Hold the Bodice with the wrong side out and an armhole facing you. With the right sides together, align the gathered end of one Sleeve with the armhole's raw edge (the ungathered end of the Sleeve should be inside the Bodice), pin the Sleeve around the hole, adjust the gathering to fit, and stitch the Sleeve to the Bodice around the armhole. Repeat to attach the other Sleeve to the other armhole. Ⓑ

7. Fold the bottom of one Sleeve under about ¼" (6mm) and press. Fold under again about ½" (13mm) and press again. Stitch around the top of the fold, leaving a 1" (2.5cm) opening near the seam. Cut the elastic for your desired size. Pin a large safety pin to one end of the elastic, and feed it through the casing. Be sure not to lose the other end into the Sleeve, and try not to twist the elastic while feeding it through. When you've gone around the whole Sleeve, overlap and pin the two ends

Ⓑ
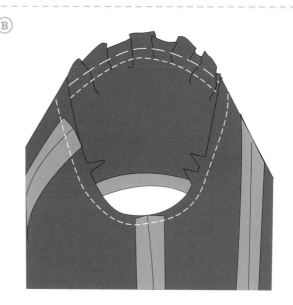

Ⓒ
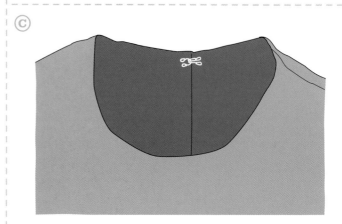

together. Zigzag stitch the two elastic ends together and close up the hole left in the Sleeve with a straight stitch. Repeat for the other Sleeve.

8. Turn the entire top right side out. Sew a hook and eye at the top of the back of the Bodice, at the base of the neck. Ⓒ

9. To finish the top, fold up the hem about ¼" (6mm) and press. Fold another ¼" (6mm), stitch it in place around the entire top, and press crisp.

Not Just for Weekends
The Sunday Dress

When you work a 9-to-5 job, weekends are precious. Half of the time you just want to lie around in loungewear eating popcorn and watching chick flicks. The other half of the time, it feels good to get decked out in something you can't quite pull off at the office. For your next Sunday brunch in the park, consider the latter.

Black eyelet has a great vintage feel but is also a bit rock-and-roll. Skipping its sweet white counterpart and going for the black version is just a little bit naughty. Also, eyelet allows you to use the gorgeous scalloped edges as your hem, so you not only skip a step in the making, but finish off the dress in major style.

FABRIC
3 yd (274.3cm) of 45" (114cm) wide, or 2¾ yd (251.5cm) of 60" (152.5cm) wide

SEAM ALLOWANCE
⅝" (16mm)

TECHNIQUES
Gathering (page 36)

Basting (page 34)

PATTERN PIECES **26** SKIRT FRONT AND BACK **28** BODICE FRONT **27** BODICE BACK **02** RUFFLE **01-A** WAIST (CUT TO 9" [23CM]) **01-A** WAIST TIE (CUT TO 25" [63.5CM])

49

Cut Out Your Dress

1. Cut out the pattern pieces for the dress in your size.

2. Lay the pattern pieces on your chosen fabric, aligning the indicated edge of each piece along the fold of the fabric (do not cut the Bodice Front pieces along the fold). Pin them in place, and cut around the perimeter of the pattern pieces. Cut two Skirt Front and Back pieces, two Bodice Back pieces, two Ruffle pieces, four Waist Tie pieces, and two Waist pieces. Cut four Bodice Front pieces, a set of two for the right front and a mirror image set of two for the left front, following the bias grain marking on the pattern.

Sew Your Dress

3. Place the right sides of the two Skirt Front and Back pieces together and stitch the side seams. Place the right sides of the two Ruffle pieces together and sew the two short ends together. Baste and gather

one of the long ends. With right sides together, pin the Ruffle to the bottom of the Skirt and stitch it in place. Hem the Ruffle by folding up the bottom about ¼" (6mm) and press. Fold another ¼" (6mm), stitch it in place around the entire Skirt, and press.

4. With right sides together, stitch two of the Waist Tie pieces together along both long edges and one short end, leaving the other short end open. Clip the corners, turn the Waist Tie right side out, and press. Repeat with the remaining two pieces.

5. Place the right sides of the two Waist pieces together. Insert the raw end of one of the Waist Ties between the Waist pieces, aligning the Waist Tie's raw end with the Waist pieces' short ends. Center the short end of the Tie on the short end of the Waist pieces. Pin the Tie in place and stitch the Waist and the Waist Tie together along the short end. Repeat to add the remaining Waist Tie to the other side of the Waist.

6. With right sides together, pin the Waist to the Skirt, adjust the gathering to fit the Waist, and stitch. Keep the Waist Tie out of the way while sewing.

7. With right sides facing, stitch two of the Bodice Front pieces together by sewing up the long sloping curve, around the pointed shoulder tie, and down the armhole. Do not stitch down the side seam. Repeat with the remaining Bodice Front pieces. With right sides together, stitch the two Bodice Back pieces together. Starting at the seam under one armhole, sew around the curve, up the shoulder tie, around the back of the neck, up to the other shoulder tie point, and back down to under the armhole. Again, do not stitch down the side seam. Clip any curved seams that are not lying flat, turn all three Bodice sets right side out, and press.

8. Lay one Bodice Front set on top of the Bodice Back, with the insides facing. Lift the top set of Bodice pieces to face right sides together along the side seam. This creates a straight line down the inside of the side seam. Pin and stitch. Lower the Bodice pieces. Press. Repeat on other side.

9. Overlap the two Bodice Front pieces, lining up with the side seams and matching the width of the Waist; pin; and baste together to hold them in place. With right sides facing, pin the entire Bodice to the Waist and stitch.

10. Fit the dress on your body and tie the shoulders to fit. Wrap the belt around and tie.

Ⓐ

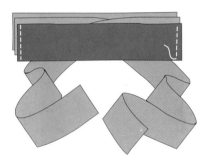

51

Ⓑ

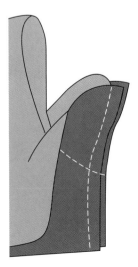

FABRIC
2½ yd (229cm) of 45" (114cm) wide, or 2 yd (183cm) of 60" (152.5cm) wide

NOTIONS
½" (13mm) elastic—Small: 25" (63.5cm); Medium: 27" (68.5cm); Large: 29" (74cm)

SEAM ALLOWANCE
⅝" (16mm)

TECHNIQUES
Casings and inserting elastic (page 36)

You Spin Me 'Round
The Modern Circle Skirt

A great chameleon for every modern girl's wardrobe is a circle skirt. The circle skirt is different from an A-line skirt in that it is literally cut in a circle, so it is fuller, like a poodle skirt or a cheerleader skirt. But trust me, yours will be much cooler.

It is quite possibly one of the easiest garments to make, but if you change up the fabric, make it longer or shorter, or add a bottom ruffle or another type of trim, you can make hundreds of these for your closet, and no one would be the wiser. I made this one from a black vintage-inspired tropical print, placed it on the hip, and topped it off with a wide belt. This helps cover the elastic waistband and gives it a clean finish.

PATTERN PIECE 22 SKIRT

Cut Out Your Skirt

1. Cut out the pattern piece for the skirt in your size.
2. Fold the fabric crosswise instead of selvage-to-selvage. Lay the Skirt piece on the fold of your fabric, pin it in place, and cut one piece out around the perimeter of the pattern piece.

Sew Your Skirt

3. Fold the Skirt in half crosswise, with right sides together, and stitch up the seam.
4. To form the waistband, fold the waist of the Skirt down about ¼" (6mm) and press. Fold again about 1" (2.5cm), and press again.
5. Starting at the side seam, stitch around the bottom of the fold, leaving a 1" (2.5cm) opening near the seam. Cut the elastic to your desired size. Pin a large safety pin to one end of the elastic, and feed it through the casing. Be sure not to lose the other end into the waist, and try not to twist the elastic while feeding it through. When you've gone around the whole waist, overlap and pin the two ends of the elastic together. Zigzag stitch the two elastic ends together, and close up the hole left in the waist with a straight stitch.
6. To finish the Skirt, fold up the hem about ¼" (6mm) and press. Fold another ¼" (6mm), stitch it in place around the entire Skirt, and press crisp.

FABRIC
2¾ yd (251.5cm) of
45" (114cm) wide, or
1¾ yd (160cm) of 60"
(152.5cm) wide

NOTIONS
40" (101.5cm) length of
½" (13mm) double-fold
bias tape, purchased
or handmade

SEAM ALLOWANCE
⅝" (16mm)

TECHNIQUES
Making handmade bias tape
(page 39)

Applying bias tape (page 39)

Gathering (page 36)

Basting (page 34)

Tie belt (page 30)

Working the Late Shift
Tie Shoulder Shift Dress

Here's your chance: Your friends have invited you to a cool underground spot, and you need something to wear. Why risk showing up in something your friends—or worse, your enemies—might be wearing? Show up in your own fabulous creation. This shift dress has a gathered neckline that you can tighten or loosen as much as you want, using the tie inserted to the neck.

I chose a sexy yet springtime-appropriate silk print with black, pink, and light blue flowers with a contrasting black silk tie bow at the neck. You can choose anything from lightweight cotton to satin or silk. Just be sure to choose something soft that will gather around your neck nicely. Scrunch up the fabric you're considering and see how it will look. And when you're done, bust it out for that night on the town.

PATTERN PIECES 09 DRESS FRONT 08 DRESS BACK 13 FRONT NECK BAND 14 BACK NECK BAND 03 BIAS TAPE (OPTIONAL) 01-A TIE BELT (CUT TO 22" [56CM])

Cut Out Your Dress

1. Cut out the pattern pieces for the dress in your size.
2. Lay the pattern pieces on your chosen fabric, aligning the indicated edge of each piece along the fold of the fabric. Pin them in place, and cut around the perimeter of the pattern pieces. Cut one Dress Front piece, one Dress Back piece, two Tie Belt pieces, two Front Neck Band pieces, and two Back Neck Band pieces. One set of Neck Band pieces will the Neck Band Facing, which will be on the inside of the dress. If you are making your own bias tape (page 39), use pattern piece 03 to cut one 40" (101.5cm) or two 20" (51cm) bias tape strips for the armholes.

Sew Your Dress

3. Place the right sides of the Dress Front and the Dress Back together and stitch the side seams. Baste and gather the top edge of both the Dress Front and the Dress Back.
4. Using either handmade bias tape or purchased double-fold bias tape, place the center fold of the tape around the edge of the armholes and stitch in place. Cut off any excess length.
5. With right sides together, stitch one Front Neck Band and one Back Neck Band together at one of the short ends. On the other side, fold one of the short ends in ¼" (6mm), wrong sides together, and press. Fold in another ¼" (6mm) and stitch in place. Repeat on the other short end. Pin the two ends

together. With right sides together, and lining up the markings on the pattern pieces, pin the Dress Front and Dress Back to the Neck Band. Adjust the gathering on the Dress to fit the markings if needed. Stitch the Neck Band in place, clip curved seams, and press the seams up toward the neck band. Press the side of the Neck Band up to match the seam allowance. Ⓐ

6. With right sides together, stitch the other Front Neck Band Facing and Back Neck Band Facing together at both short ends. Fold the outside edge in ¼" (6mm), wrong sides together, and press. Fold in another ¼" (6mm) and press. With right sides together, place the Neck Band Facing on top of the Neck Band, aligning the seams. Be careful to keep the open ends of the Neck Band together when stitching over the seam in the Neck Band with the opening. Stitch the Bands together around the inner circle. Ⓑ Clip curved seams. Fold the Neck Band Facing to the inside of the Dress, trapping the gathered seams between the Neck Band and the Facing; pin in place; and press. On the outside of your dress, topstitch the Neck Band around the whole Dress to secure it to the Neck Band Facing. Then, topstitch the inner circle of the Neck Band (closest to your neck). Ⓒ

7. To form the Tie Belt, with right sides together, sew the two Tie Belt strips together at one short end. Fold in half lengthwise, with right sides together, and stitch around both short ends and one long edge. Stitch the other long edge, leaving an opening about 2" (5cm) wide. Clip the corners of the seams, turn the Tie right side out through the opening, and press crisp. Fold the seam allowance into the opening, press, and slipstitch closed. Pin a large safety pin

to one end of the Tie Belt and feed it into the hole in the Neck Band. Push it through the entire Neck Band and back out the same hole.

8. To finish the Dress, fold up the hem about ¼" (6mm) and press. Fold another ¼" (6mm), stitch it in place around the entire Dress, and press crisp.

Ⓐ

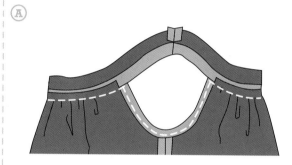

Ⓑ

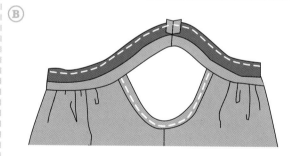

Ⓒ

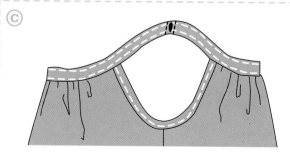

56

Singing in the Rain
The Trench

In the springtime, when it starts to rain, don't you secretly love it? It washes away all the dirt and grime that winter has built up on the streets, cleaning everything anew. Plus, once it starts to rain, that usually means that it is done snowing. Come March, that feels pretty darn good. And rain is the perfect excuse to bust out that adorable trench coat you made over the winter just for this occasion.

    The trench coat is a garment where you can really go wild with prints. It is somehow completely acceptable to have a brightly colored print trench over your classic black urban uniform. I chose a medium weight cotton with a great retro print. Stick to a medium weight fabric, and your coat will fit just right. Also, there are optional patch pockets, or you can wear it with a belt, like the Jacket on page 98.

FABRIC
2½ yd (229cm) of 45" (114cm) wide, or 1¾ yd (160cm) of 60" (152.5cm) wide

NOTIONS
94" (239cm) of handmade bias tape or store-bought ½" (13mm) double-fold bias tape

SEAM ALLOWANCE
⅝" (16mm)

TECHNIQUES
Making handmade bias tape (page 39)

Applying bias tape (page 39)

Patch pockets (page 35)

PATTERN PIECES **25** JACKET FRONT **24** JACKET BACK
23 SLEEVE **16** POCKET (OPTIONAL) **03** BIAS TAPE (OPTIONAL)

57

Cut Out Your Trench Coat

1. Cut out the pattern pieces for the trench and the optional pockets in your size.
2. Lay the pattern pieces on your chosen fabric, aligning the indicated edge of each piece along the fold of the fabric (do not cut the Sleeve or Jacket Front piece along the fold). Pin them in place, and cut around the perimeter of the pattern pieces. Cut out two Jacket Front pieces, one Jacket Back piece, and two Sleeve pieces. If you would like your coat to have pockets, also cut two Patch Pocket pieces.

Ⓐ

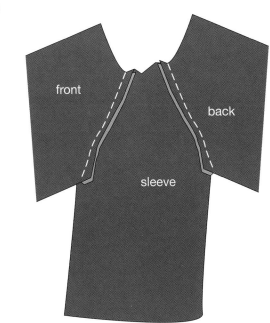

front

back

sleeve

Sew Your Trench Coat

3. With right sides together, stitch the front edge of one Sleeve piece (it is marked front) to one Jacket Front piece at the shoulder. Repeat with the other Jacket Front and Sleeve. Ⓐ

4. With right sides together, stitch the back edge of one Sleeve piece (marked back) to one Jacket Back piece at the shoulder. Repeat with the other side of the Jacket Back piece.

5. Place the trench flat with right sides together, with the Front and Back pieces facing each other and the Sleeves folded in half. Pin up the side seam of the trench, under the arm, and down the Sleeve to the cuff and stitch in place. Repeat on the other side of the jacket. Ⓑ

6. Line up the bias tape you have made or purchased along the front opening of the trench on both the left-hand side and the right-hand side, and sew the tape in place. Pin the bias tape for the neck in place, leaving equal excess bias tape on both sides. Fold the excess under and pin. Stitch in place.

7. To finish the trench, fold up the hem, including the bias tape, about ¼" (6mm) and press. Fold another ¼" (6mm), stitch it in place around the entire trench, and press crisp. Fold up the cuffs on the Sleeves in the same way and stitch.

8. To make the optional Pockets, follow the instructions in the Techniques section (page 35).

9. Following the marks on the pattern piece, pin the Pocket in place on the trench and stitch.

59

Ⓑ

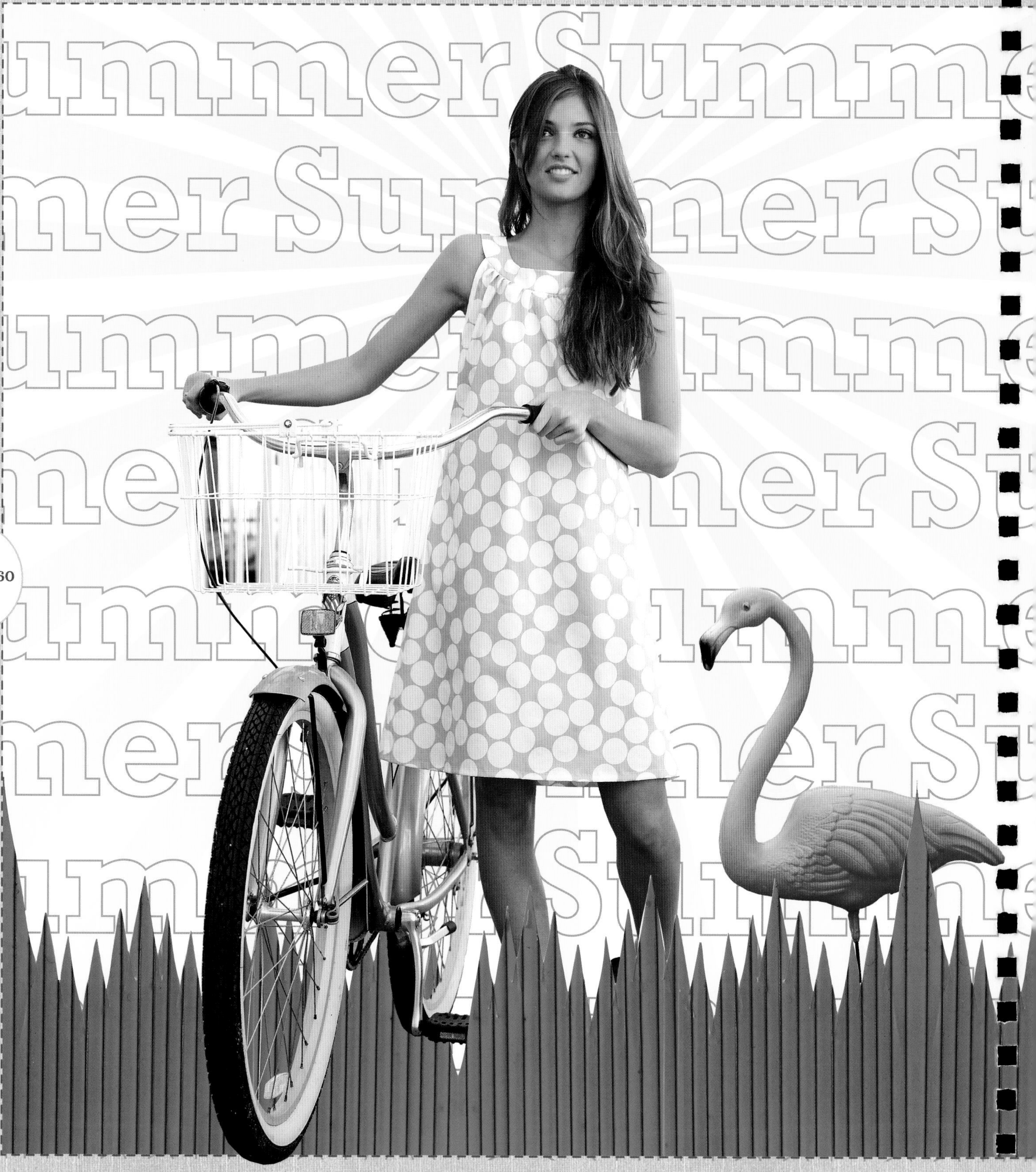

Summer

Ahhh, summer. Summer brings so much to mind—summer break, summer vacation, summer camp, summer romance. Oh, and of course, summer heat! Sure, we're happy that it is finally warm enough to wear flip flops and sleeveless dresses, but it can be hot and humid too. So this is the perfect time of year to wear as little as you can get away with, in order to look good but stay cool.

In this summer collection is a range of garments that will look great on the shore, in the park, or out on the town. Included are a fun strapless dress, a classic A-line skirt, a retro shift dress, a sweet sundress, a crisp and classic wrap top, and a date dress perfect for that summer night out. As is true for the clothes in the other seasons, these can be worn at any time of year.

Summer is also a great time of year for color. You can get away with almost anything. Hot pink, black, bright lime green, chocolate brown, and white all look appropriate this time of year. It's the only time you can really do this, so don't hold back, because summer always goes faster than you think it will, and before you know it, the leaves are falling off the trees.

Going to the Shore
The Sundress

Oh, thank goodness it's summer! It's time to hit the beach. You can wear this dress anywhere, of course, but the beach is what summer vacations are all about—sun, surf, sand. And for that, you'll need a sundress. This one is made especially adorable by the addition of ruffles sewn into the straps at the shoulders (which you can certainly skip if ruffles aren't your thing).

I used lightweight cotton in a fun retro print with contrasting black bust casing and straps. Choose something that flows well and is relatively lightweight, but feel free to mix and match the pieces. The straps can be their own color, as can the ruffles. There are really no rules here, especially since it's summer, and let's face it, almost anything goes this time of year.

FABRIC
2¾ yd (251.5cm) of
45" (114cm) wide, or
2 yd (183cm) of 60"
(152.5cm) wide

SEAM ALLOWANCE
⅝" (16mm)

TECHNIQUES
Gathering (page 36)

Basting (page 34)

PATTERN PIECES 10 DRESS FRONT AND BACK 01-A FRONT AND BACK CASING (CUT TO 9" [23CM]) 01-B SHOULDER STRAPS (CUT TO 16" [40.5CM]) 15 SHOULDER RUFFLE 02 RUFFLE

Cut Out Your Dress

1. Cut out the pattern pieces for the dress in your size.

2. Lay the pattern pieces on your chosen fabric, aligning the indicated edge of each piece along the fold of the fabric. Pin them in place, and cut around the perimeter of the pattern pieces. Cut two Dress Front and Back pieces, two Dress Ruffle pieces, and four Shoulder Ruffle pieces. Use pattern piece 01-A to cut out two pieces for the Front and Back Casing and piece 01-B to cut out two pieces for the Shoulder Straps.

Sew Your Dress

3. Place the right sides of the two Dress Front and Back pieces together, and stitch the side seams.

4. With right sides together, sew both short ends of the Bust Casing Front and Back pieces together. Turn the Bust Casing right side out, fold it in half lengthwise with wrong sides together, and press.

5. Baste around the top of the Dress and gather to fit the casing length.

6. Place the right sides of two Shoulder Ruffle pieces together, and stitch up one short end, across the arch, and down the other short end. Clip curves, turn right side out, and press crisp. Repeat with the remaining two Shoulder Ruffle pieces.

7. Baste and gather the long end of each Shoulder Ruffle. With right sides up and the gathered edge of one Shoulder Ruffle aligned with one long edge of a Shoulder Strap, place the Shoulder Ruffle on top of the Shoulder Strap, leaving 3" (7.5cm) between the short end of the Shoulder Ruffle and the short

end of the Shoulder Strap. Stitch the Shoulder Ruffle in place. 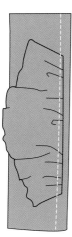 Turn the Shoulder Strap over, wrong side up, and fold the edge with the Shoulder Ruffle stitched to it in ½" (13mm). Fold the opposite edge in ½" (13mm). Lining up the two folded sides, fold the Shoulder Strap in half lengthwise with right sides out, and press. Stitch the folded edges of the Shoulder Strap together, making sure to catch the Shoulder Ruffle in the stitching. Repeat for the remaining Shoulder Ruffle and Shoulder Strap.

8. Starting at one of the side seams, and with right sides together, pin the Bust Casing to the dress, lining up raw edges and adjusting the gathering to fit if necessary. Pin the Straps to the Bust Casing 4" (10cm) from the side seams, lining up the bottom edge of the Strap with the bottom of the Casing. Stitch the Casing and Straps to the dress all at once. Secure the Straps by topstitching at the top of the Casing.

9. Place the right sides of the two Dress Ruffle pieces together and stitch up both pairs of short ends.

Baste around the top of one of the long edges of the Ruffle. Gather the Ruffle, line up the side seams, pin it to the bottom of the Dress with right sides together, and sew it in place.

10. To finish, fold up the hem of the Ruffle about ¼" (6mm) and press. Fold another ¼" (6mm), stitch it in place around the entire Skirt, and press crisp.

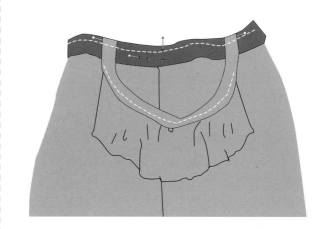

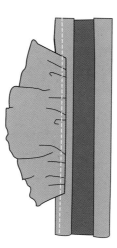

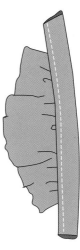

64

You're So Shifty
The Retro Shift Dress

I've always loved 1960s shift dresses. They are timeless, fun, and endlessly youthful. So I thought that this collection needed something with that kind of spirit. This shift dress has a modern feel, but retains that fun of days gone by, especially when it is made in this lime polka dot print.

A lightweight or medium weight cotton blend is the best choice for this dress. Satin and silk would work, too, if you're looking to twist this into something else completely. Which is fine by me. That's the nature of making it yourself—you're in the driver's seat.

FABRIC
2½ yd (229cm) of 45" (114cm) wide, or 1½ yd (137cm) of 60" (152.5cm) wide

NOTIONS
40" (101.5cm) length of ½" (13mm) double-fold bias tape, purchased or handmade

SEAM ALLOWANCE
⅝" (16mm)

TECHNIQUES
Making handmade bias tape (page 39)

Applying bias tape (page 39)

Gathering (page 36)

Basting (page 34)

PATTERN PIECES 09 DRESS FRONT 08 DRESS BACK 13 FRONT NECK BAND 14 BACK NECK BAND 03 BIAS TAPE (OPTIONAL)

65

Cut Out Your Dress

1. Cut out the pattern pieces for the dress in your size.

2. Lay the pattern pieces on your chosen fabric, aligning the indicated edge of each piece along the fold of the fabric. Pin them in place, and cut around the perimeter of the pattern pieces. Cut one Dress Front piece, one Dress Back piece, two Front Neck Band pieces, and two Back Neck Band pieces. One set of Neck Band pieces will be the Neck Band Facing set, which will be on the inside of the dress. If you are making your own bias tape (page 39), use pattern piece 03 to cut one 40" (101.5cm) or two 20" (51cm) bias tape strips for the armholes.

Sew Your Dress

3. Place the right sides of the Dress Front and the Dress Back together and stitch the side seams. Baste and gather the top edge of both the Dress Front and the Dress Back.

4. Using either handmade bias tape or purchased double-fold bias tape, place the center fold of the tape around the edge of the armholes and stitch in place. Cut off any excess length.

5. With right sides together, stitch one Front Neck Band and one Back Neck Band together at both short ends. With right sides together, and lining up the markings on the pattern pieces, pin the Dress Front and Dress Back to the Neck Band. Adjust the gathering on the dress to fit the markings if needed. Stitch the Neck Band in place, clip curved seams, and press the seams up toward the Neck Band. Press the side of the Neck Band up to match the seam allowance.

6. With right sides together, stitch the other Front Neck Band Facing and the Back Neck Band Facing together at both short ends. Fold the outside edge in ¼" (6mm), wrong sides together, and press. Fold in another ¼" (6mm) and press. With right sides together, place the Neck Band Facing on top of the Neck Band, aligning the seams. Stitch the bands together around the inner circle. Clip curved seams. Fold the Neck Band Facing to the inside of the dress, trapping the gathered seams between the Neck Band and the Facing; pin in place; and press. On the outside of your dress, topstitch the Neck Band around the whole dress to secure it to the Neck Band Facing. Then, topstitch the inner circle of the Neck Band (closest to your neck).

7. To finish the dress, fold up the hem about ¼" (6mm) and press. Fold another ¼" (6mm), stitch it in place around the entire dress, and press crisp.

Ⓐ

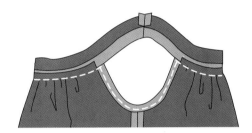

Ⓑ

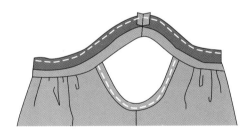

Ⓒ

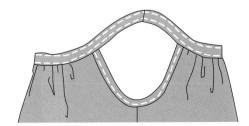

67

FABRIC

2 yd (183cm) of 45" (114cm) wide, or 2 yd (183cm) of 60" (152.5cm) wide

NOTIONS

½" (13mm) elastic—Small: 25" (63.5cm); Medium: 27" (68.5cm); Large: 29" (74cm)

SEAM ALLOWANCE

⅝" (16mm)

TECHNIQUES

Casings and inserting elastic (page 36)

Gathering (page 36)

Basting (page 34)

68

A is for More Than Just Apples

The A-line Skirt

Much like the Modern Circle Skirt on page 52, the A-line skirt is a great basic for every wardrobe. No matter what your personal style, the A-line skirt can be modified to suit your tastes. The make up of an A-line skirt is basically two triangles sewn together with the top point chopped off.

Suitable for every body type, the version I made has a pretty ruffle at the hem. But yours doesn't have to. If you don't want a ruffle, just skip step 6 and go straight to hemming.

I chose a lightweight black and gray stripe, but you can pick whatever you like: black silk with a lace ruffle, retro pink flowers with no ruffle—the possibilities are endless. What's important is that you choose lightweight or medium weight fabric. If you pick something too heavy and thick, the skirt will stick out from the waist, which might be unflattering.

PATTERN PIECES 26 SKIRT FRONT AND BACK 02 RUFFLE

Cut Out Your Skirt

1. Cut out the pattern pieces for the skirt in your size.
2. Lay the pattern pieces on your chosen fabric, aligning the indicated edge of each piece along the fold of the fabric. Pin them in place, and cut around the perimeter of the pattern pieces. Cut out two Skirt Front and Back pieces and two Ruffle pieces.

Sew Your Skirt

3. Place the right sides of the two Skirt Front and Back pieces together and stitch the side seams.

4. To form the waistband, fold the waist of the Skirt down about ¼" (6mm) and press. Fold again about 1" (2.5cm) and press again.
5. Starting at one of the side seams, stitch around the bottom of the fold, leaving a 1" (2.5cm) opening near the seam. Cut the elastic to your desired size. Pin a large safety pin to one end of the elastic, and feed it through the casing. Be sure not to lose the other end into the waist, and try not to twist the elastic while feeding it through. When you've gone around the whole waist, pin the two ends of the elastic together. Zigzag stitch the two elastic

ends together and close up the hole left in the waistband with a straight stitch.

6. Place the right sides of the two Ruffle pieces together and stitch up both pairs of short ends. Baste around the top of one of the long edges of the Ruffle. Gather the Ruffle, pin it to the bottom of the Skirt with right sides together, and sew it in place.

7. To finish the Skirt, fold up the hem of the Ruffle about ¼" (6mm) and press. Fold another ¼" (6mm), stitch it in place around the entire Ruffle, and press crisp.

Classic with a Twist
The Wrap Top

Everyone needs a crisp white cotton top in their collection. But there's no need to have only boring white button-down collared shirts. You're far more interesting than that! Not only is this shirt classic, but it is also flattering and sexy.

I picked a soft white cotton Swiss dot fabric with little raised dots on it. It looks sweet and feminine, but when worn in this way there's nothing innocent about it. I also chose to trim the top with solid white bias tape. You can choose to make your own to match, omit it all together, or get crazy and use a contrasting trim. Wouldn't this top look great if that trim were black? Or even better, you can make your own bias tape in a vintage plaid or polka dot. No one could call your white shirt boring after that.

FABRIC
1½ yd (137cm) of 45" (114cm) wide, or 1¼ yd (114cm) of 60" (152.5cm) wide

NOTIONS
60" (152.5cm) of ½" (13mm) double-fold bias tape (optional)

¼" (6mm) elastic—Small: 12" (30.5cm); Medium: 13½" (34.5cm); Large: 15" (38cm)

SEAM ALLOWANCE
⅝" (16mm)

TECHNIQUES
Casings and inserting elastic (page 36)

Stitching curves (page 33)

Making handmade bias tape (page 39)

Applying bias tape (page 39)

Gathering (page 36)

Basting (page 34)

71

PATTERN PIECES 18 BODICE FRONT 19 BODICE FRONT SIDE 17 SLEEVE 21 BODICE BACK 20 BODICE BACK SIDE 01-A WAIST TIES (CUT TO 22" [56CM]) 03 BIAS TAPE (OPTIONAL)

Cut Out Your Top
1. Cut out the pattern pieces for the top in your size.
2. Lay out the pattern pieces on your fabric following the grain and fold markings on the pattern. Pin them in place, and cut around the perimeter of each pattern piece. Cut two Bodice Front pieces, two Bodice Front Side pieces, two Sleeve pieces, and two Bodice Back Side pieces. Cut one Bodice Back piece and four Waist Tie pieces on the fold of your fabric. If you choose to make bias tape, use pattern piece 03 and follow the directions in the Techniques section (page 39).

(A)

(B)

(C)

Sew Your Top

3. With right sides together and the notches on the patterns aligned, stitch the Bodice Front and Bodice Front Side pieces together. (A) Sewing this front curve can be a bit tricky, but if you just turn the piece along as you sew, it will turn out great. Sew the Bodice Back and Bodice Back Side pieces together in the same way. (B)

4. With right sides together, stitch the Bodice Front to the Bodice Back at the shoulder seam.

5. With right sides facing, stitch the Bodice Back to the Bodice Front at the side seams, leaving an opening between the two dots marked on the pattern piece. Be sure to backstitch at the opening to secure the seam.

6. Press open the side seam with the opening. Fold the seam around the opening under ¼" (6mm) and topstitch all the way around the hole to keep it open. (C)

7. Fold each Sleeve piece in half crosswise, with right sides together, and stitch the short seams together. Baste around the top of the Sleeve between the two dots on the Sleeve pattern piece, and gather. Hold the Bodice with the wrong side out and an armhole facing you. With the right sides together, align the gathered end of one Sleeve with the armhole's raw edge, lining up the seam in the Sleeve with the side seam in the Bodice (the ungathered end of the Sleeve should be inside the Bodice). Pin the Sleeve in the armhole, adjust the gathering to fit, and stitch the Sleeve to the Bodice around the armhole. (D) Repeat to attach the other Sleeve to the other armhole. Turn the Bodice and the Sleeves right side out.

73

8. Fold the bottom of the Sleeve under about ¼" (6mm) and press. Fold under again about ½" (13mm) and press again. Stitch around the top of the fold, leaving a 1" (2.5cm) opening near the seam. Cut the elastic for your desired size. Pin a large safety pin to one end of the elastic, and feed it through the casing. Be sure not to lose the other end into the Sleeve, and try not to twist the elastic while feeding it through. When you've gone around the whole Sleeve, overlap the two ends and pin. Zigzag stitch the two elastic ends together and close up the hole left in the Sleeve with a straight stitch.

9. If you are not using bias tape, fold and press the sides of the Bodice and neck under ¼" (6mm). Fold under and press another ¼" (6mm) and stitch. If you are using either handmade bias tape or purchased double-fold bias tape, line up the raw end of the bias tape at the hem in the front of the top. Starting there, pin the tape up one side of the Bodice, around the neck, and back down the other side of the Bodice to the bottom of the top, ending at the hem opposite of where you started. Stitch in place.

10. With right sides together, stitch two of the Waist Tie pieces together along both long edges and one of the short ends, leaving the other short end open. Turn the Waist Tie right side out, and press flat. Fold the seam allowance on the raw end into the Waist Tie and press. Repeat with the remaining two Waist Tie pieces.

11. Pin the unfinished end of the Waist Tie to the inside of the Bodice Front, between the two dots on the pattern. Stitch in place. Ⓔ Repeat with the remaining Waist Tie and Bodice Front.

74

12. To finish the top, fold up the hem—including the bias tape, if used—about ¼" (6mm) and press. Fold another ¼" (6mm), and stitch in place around the entire top.

Ⓓ

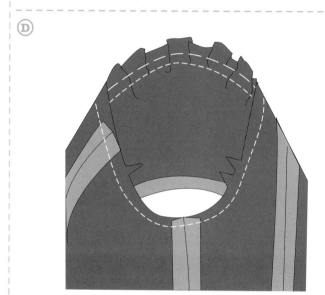

Ⓔ

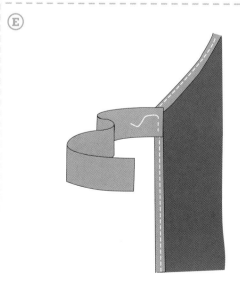

Cutting Ties
The Strapless Dress

I love the shape of this dress. It's a classic strapless dress finished with elastic at the waist and a sweet ruffle at the hem. The possibilities are so unbelievably endless. Much like the rest of projects in this book, this dress can be made in a thousand different ways, and your friends would never know that you used the same pattern to make them all.

I chose to illustrate how each pattern piece can be made from different fabrics by selecting variegated colors of the same family—red, bright pink, and light pink. But much like other projects, you can choose an endless host of options: black top and skirt with no ruffle, yellow top with a green and yellow floral skirt and ruffle, or anything in between. Just stick to something lightweight or medium weight, and the rest is up to you.

FABRIC
2¼ yd (205.7cm) of 45" (114cm) wide, or 1¾ yd (160cm) of 60" (152.5cm) wide

NOTIONS
½" (13mm) elastic for bust—Small: 27" (68.5cm); Medium: 29" (74cm); Large: 31" (79cm)

½" (13mm) elastic for waist—Small: 25" (63.5cm); Medium: 27" (68.5cm); Large: 29" (74cm)

SEAM ALLOWANCE
⅝" (16mm)

TECHNIQUES
Casings and inserting elastic (page 36)

Gathering (page 36)

Basting (page 34)

77

PATTERN PIECES 26 SKIRT FRONT AND BACK 30 BODICE FRONT 29 BODICE BACK 02 RUFFLE

Cut Out Your Dress

1. Cut out the pattern pieces for the dress in your size.
2. Lay the pattern pieces on your chosen fabric, aligning the indicated edge of each piece along the fold of the fabric. Pin them in place, and cut around the perimeter of the pattern pieces. Cut out two Skirt Front and Back pieces, one Bodice Front piece, one Bodice Back piece, and two Ruffle pieces.

Sew Your Dress

3. Place the right sides of the Skirt Front and Back pieces together and stitch the side seams.

4. Place the right sides of the Bodice Front and Bodice Back together and stitch the side seams. Fold down the top of the Bodice ¼" (6mm) and press. Fold again about 1" (2.5cm) and press. Starting at one of the side seams, stitch around the bottom of the fold, leaving a 1" (2.5cm) opening near the seam where you started.

5. Cut elastic for your desired bust size. Pin a large safety pin to one end of the elastic, and feed it through the casing created in the previous step. Be sure not to lose the other end into the casing, and try not to twist the elastic while feeding it through. When you've gone around the bust, pin the two

ends of the elastic together. Zigzag stitch the two elastic ends together and close up the hole left in the Bodice with a straight stitch.

6. With right sides together, pin the bottom of the Bodice to the top of the Skirt, lining up the side seams. Stitch 1¼" (3cm) below the edge where the Skirt and Bodice meet. Stitch again ½" (13mm) below the edge, leaving a 1" (2.5cm) opening at the side seam where you started.

7. Cut elastic for your desired waist size and insert elastic the same way you did for the bust in step 5.

Close the hole left in the Skirt with a straight stitch.

8. To make the bottom Ruffle, place the right sides of the two Ruffle pieces together and sew the two short ends together. Baste around one of the long sides and gather the Ruffle to fit onto the bottom of the Skirt. With right sides together, pin the Ruffle to the bottom of the Skirt and stitch.

9. To finish the dress, hem the Ruffle by folding up the bottom about ¼" (6mm), and then press. Fold another ¼" (6mm), stitch it in place around the entire dress, and press crisp.

Pencil Me In
The Date Dress

You're meeting a special someone for drinks after work, so you want to wear something that can swing both ways. This dress can be hidden under a tailored jacket by day, but by night, it feels so liberating to lose that layer. That's one thing that's so great about summer: The freedom of going out on the town in almost nothing. And no one will judge you for it, especially since it can be 80 degrees at 10 p.m. Why would you even consider wearing anything more?

For this dress, I picked a beautiful silk with a chocolate brown and cream print. For the straps and belt, a contrasting black brings this up to a higher level of sophistication. You can pick what you like; just make sure it is lightweight and flowy. No one should fear this dress, as it looks great on every kind of body.

FABRIC
2½ yd (229cm) of 45" (114cm) wide, or 1½ yd (137cm) of 60" (152.5cm) wide

SEAM ALLOWANCE
⅝" (16mm)

TECHNIQUES
Tie belt (page 30)

Gathering (page 36)

Basting (page 34)

PATTERN PIECES 10 DRESS FRONT AND BACK 01-A FRONT AND BACK CASING (CUT AT 9" [23CM]) 01-B SHOULDER STRAPS (CUT AT 16" [40.5CM]) 01-A TIE BELT (CUT AT 22" [56CM])

79

Cut Out Your Dress

1. Cut out the pattern pieces for the dress in your size.

2. Lay the pattern pieces on your chosen fabric, aligning the indicated edge of each piece along the fold of the fabric. Pin them in place, and cut around the perimeter of the pattern pieces. Cut out two Dress Front and Back pieces, two Front and Back Casing pieces, two Shoulder Strap pieces, and four Tie Belt pieces.

Sew Your Dress

3. Place the right sides of the two Dress Front and Back pieces together and stitch the side seams.

4. With right sides together, sew the short ends of the

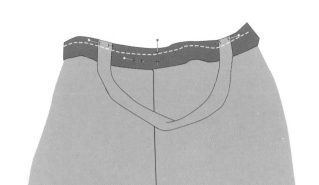

two Front and Back Casing pieces together. Fold in half lengthwise, right sides out, and press.

5. Baste around the top of the dress, and gather to fit the Casing. With right sides together, line up raw ends, and pin the dress to the Casing.

6. To make the Straps, fold each Shoulder Strap piece in half lengthwise, with right sides together. Stitch along the long open end of the Straps, leaving the two short ends open. Turn right side out and press.

7. Pin each Strap to the Casing, 4" (10cm) from the side seams on both the Casing Front and the Casing Back, lining up the bottom edge of the strap with the bottom of the Casing. Stitch the Casing and the Straps to the dress all at once. Ⓐ Secure the Straps by topstitching at the top of the Casing. Ⓑ

8. To make the Tie Belt, with right sides together, sew two of the Tie Belt strips together at a short end. Repeat with the remaining strips. With these two long strips right sides together, stitch both short ends and one long edge. Stitch the other long edge, leaving an opening about 2" (5cm) wide. Clip the corners of the seams, turn the tie right side out through that opening, and press crisp. Fold the seam allowance into the opening, press, and slipstitch closed.

9. To finish the dress, fold up the hem about ¼" (6mm) and press. Fold another ¼" (6mm), stitch it in place around the entire dress, and press crisp.

Ⓐ

Ⓑ

81

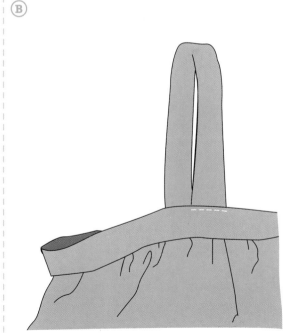

Fall

Everyone thinks of fall as a return to business—back to school, back to work, back to reality. Summer's over, and you have mixed feelings about that. On the one hand, you've grown tired of the heat and humidity, but on the other hand, summer went fast, and you didn't get to do nearly as much as you wanted to. Hopefully, as the leaves start to fall off the trees, you will begin to get excited about curling up in a big fuzzy sweater and wearing tights again.

With this collection, I've designed a variety of pieces that work with the range of temperatures that fall can give you. There's a baby doll dress, a classic wrap skirt, a sundress for that rare Indian summer day, a strapless cocktail dress, a sexy little black dress, and a crisp jacket that is perfect for layering.

The key to fall is mixing the right colors together. Earth tones, black, and rich, deep hues look great with punches of red, yellow, and pink. Mix it up and wear that little black dress with a pair of hot pink tights. Why not? Even though this season is a return to business, that doesn't mean that it has to be business as usual, especially when you're going out on the town.

Here Comes the Sun
The Indian Summer Dress

Oh, how glorious it is when you're convinced that summer is gone for good, and you are doomed to months and months of cold weather. Then, it happens—the Indian summer day. Out of nowhere, it is sunny and in the 70s, and you have one last chance to bust out something summery. But it isn't really right to wear light pink or white. I mean, it is after Labor Day, after all.

Because of the season, I picked an adorable dark burgundy gingham that is sweet and vintagey but also season-appropriate. If you are wearing this in the fall, I recommend sticking to similar rules of fashion, but there's nothing that says you can't make this in another color for spring or summer. Or, for that matter, in black with lace straps for a holiday party. Just stick to a lightweight or medium weight silk, satin, cotton, or blend, and you can pull it off any time of year.

FABRIC
3 yd (274.3cm) of 45" (114cm) wide, or 3 yd (274.3cm) of 60" (152.5cm) wide

NOTIONS
½" (13mm) elastic for waist—Small: 25" (63.5cm); Medium: 27" (68.5cm); Large: 29" (74cm)

½" (13mm) elastic for bust—Small: 27" (68.5cm); Medium: 29" (74cm); Large: 31" (79cm)

SEAM ALLOWANCE
⅝" (16mm)

TECHNIQUES
Casings and inserting elastic (page 36)

85

PATTERN PIECES 22 SKIRT 30 BODICE FRONT 29 BODICE BACK 01-A SHOULDER STRAPS (CUT AT 9" [23CM])

Cut Out Your Dress

1. Cut out the pattern pieces for the dress in your size.

2. Fold the fabric crosswise instead of selvage-to-selvage. Lay the pattern pieces on your chosen fabric, aligning the indicated edge of each piece along the fold of the fabric. Pin them in place, and cut around the perimeter of the pattern pieces. Cut one Skirt piece, one Bodice Front piece, one Bodice Back piece, and four Shoulder Strap pieces.

Sew Your Dress

3. Fold the Skirt in half crosswise, with right sides together, and stitch up the seam of the Skirt.

4. Place the Bodice Front on the Bodice Back,

with right sides together, and sew the two side seams. To form the casing, fold down the top of the Bodice ¼" (6mm), press, fold again about 1" (2.5cm), and press.

5. With right sides together, fold all of the Shoulder Strap pieces in half lengthwise. Stitch along the long open edge and one of the short ends. Turn right side out and press.

6. Pin two Shoulder Straps to the Bodice Front, each 4" (10cm) from one of the side seams, lining up the raw edge with the bottom of the casing fold. Repeat to add Shoulder Straps to the Bodice Back.

7. Starting at one of the side seams, stitch around the bottom of the casing fold, stitching over the

four Straps, and leaving a 1" (2.5cm) opening at the seam where you started. Before inserting the elastic, topstitch across each Strap at the top of the Bodice to secure the Straps in place. Ⓐ Be careful to stitch close to the folded edge to leave enough space for the elastic to go through the casing.

8. Cut the elastic to your desired size. Pin a large safety pin to one end of the elastic, and feed it through the casing. Be sure not to lose the other end, and try not to twist the elastic while feeding it through. When you've gone around the bust, pin the two ends of the elastic together. Zigzag stitch the two elastic ends together and close up the hole left in the Bodice with a straight stitch.

9. With right sides together, pin the bottom of the Bodice to the top of the Skirt, lining up the seam in the Skirt with one of the side seams in the Bodice. Stitch 1¼" (3cm) below the edge where the Skirt and the Bodice meet. Stitch again ½" (2cm) below the edge, leaving a 1" (2.5cm) opening at one of the Bodice side seams where you started.

10. Cut the elastic to your desired size and insert it to the waist as you did in the Bodice.

11. To finish the Skirt, fold up the hem about ¼" (6mm) and press. Fold another ¼" (6mm), stitch it in place around the entire Skirt, and press crisp.

12. Try on the dress and tie the Shoulder Ties to fit.

86

Ⓐ

Not Just for Kids
The Baby Doll Dress

How does one dress hide flaws and make you look sweet and saucy all at once? I don't know how it happens, but the baby doll dress does. So let's not question it; let's just wear it. This dress is a timeless phenomenon. It never goes out of style, and suits almost every body type.

I chose a vintage-inspired Asian floral print. Nearly every style of print will work, as long as you stick to lightweight or medium weight fabric. The nature of the baby doll is that it is meant to be full and to flow with ease. So steer clear of heavy, thick, or stiff fabrics, as you will lose the ease of the cut.

FABRIC
2¾ yd (251.5cm) of 45" (114cm) wide, or 2 yd (183cm) of 60" (152.5cm) wide

NOTIONS
¼" (6mm) elastic—Small: 12" (30.5cm); Medium: 13½" (34.5cm); Large: 15" (38cm)

1 hook and eye set

SEAM ALLOWANCE
⅝" (16mm)

TECHNIQUES
Casings and inserting elastic (page 36)

Gathering (page 36)

Basting (page 34)

PATTERN PIECES 07 DRESS FRONT AND BACK 04 BODICE FRONT 05 BODICE BACK 06 SLEEVE

Cut Out Your Dress

1. Cut out the pattern pieces for the dress in your size.
2. Lay the pattern pieces on your chosen fabric, aligning the indicated edge of each piece along the fold of the fabric (do not cut the Bodice Back pieces along the fold). Pin them in place, and cut around the perimeter of the pattern pieces. Cut two Dress Front and Back pieces, two Bodice Front pieces, and two Sleeve pieces. Cut four Bodice Back pieces, a set of two pieces for the right back and a mirror-image set of two pieces for the left back.

Sew Your Dress

3. With right sides together, stitch the right-hand Bodice Back piece to the right-hand shoulder of the Bodice Front. Repeat with the left-hand side, and then repeat this entire step to make an identical set of Bodice pieces.

4. Place the two Bodice pieces right sides together and stitch up one open center seam of the Back Bodice, around the neck, and back down the other center seam of the Back Bodice. Ⓐ Clip the seams around the curve of the neck, turn right side out, and press flat. Pin the two sides at the base of the center of the Bodice Back to keep them together. Keep them pinned in place while you attach them to the Dress Front and Back in the next step.

5. Place the right sides of the two Dress Front and Back pieces together and stitch the side seams. Baste and gather the top of the two Dress Front and Back pieces. Adjust the gather to fit the Bodice. Pin the Bodice in place, with right sides together and raw

edges and side seams aligned. Starting at one of the side seams, stitch the Bodice to the dress.

6. Fold each Sleeve piece in half crosswise, with right sides together, and stitch the short ends together. Baste around the top of each Sleeve pattern piece, between the two dots on the top of each Sleeve pattern piece, and gather. Hold the Bodice with the wrong side out and an armhole facing you. With the right sides together, align the gathered end of one Sleeve with the armhole's raw edge (the ungathered end of the Sleeve should be inside the Bodice); pin the Sleeve around the hole; adjust the gathering to fit; and stitch the Sleeve to the Bodice around the armhole. Repeat to attach the other Sleeve to the other armhole.

7. Fold the bottom of one Sleeve under about ¼" (6mm) and press. Fold under again about ½" (13mm) and press again. Stitch around the top of the fold, leaving a 1" (2.5cm) opening near the seam. Cut the elastic for your desired size. Pin a large safety pin to one end of the elastic, and feed it through the casing. Be sure not to lose the other end into the Sleeve, and try not to twist the elastic

while feeding it through. When you've gone around the whole Sleeve, overlap and pin the two ends together. Zigzag stitch the two elastic ends together and close up the hole left in the Sleeve with a straight stitch. Repeat for the other Sleeve.

8. Turn the entire dress right side out. Sew a hook and eye at the top of the Back Bodice, at the base of the neck.

9. To finish the dress, fold up the hem about ¼" (6mm) and press. Fold another ¼" (6mm), stitch it in place around the entire dress, and press crisp.

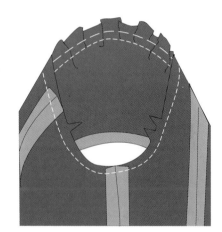

89

The ABCs of Fashion
The LBD

You don't need me to tell you that everyone should own an LBD, right? And I certainly don't need to spell it out as Little Black Dress, do I? Well, maybe I do. Okay, you really must own a little black dress. No, for real. If you don't already own one, and you have time to make only one thing in this book, this is the one. The LBD is timeless, effortless, sexy, and classic. Think Audrey Hepburn in *Breakfast at Tiffany's*. She lived in various LBDs, and you can too.

I picked a medium weight black cotton blend. Because of the drape of this dress, it is best not to pick anything too stiff or too thick, or it will hang way too far from your body and give you no shape at all. You want a lightweight or medium weight cotton, silk, satin, or blend. And this doesn't have to be your only LBD from this collection—make any of the other choices in black, and they can be LBDs too.

FABRIC
2 yd (183cm) of 45" (114cm) wide, or 1½ yd (137cm) of 60" (152.5cm) wide

SEAM ALLOWANCE
⅝" (16mm)

TECHNIQUES
Casings and inserting elastic (page 36)

Gathering (page 36)

Basting (page 34)

91

PATTERN PIECES 10 DRESS FRONT AND BACK 01-B SHOULDER STRAPS (CUT TO 9½" [24CM]) 01-A FRONT AND BACK CASING (CUT TO 9" [23CM])

Cut Out Your Dress

1. Cut out the pattern pieces for the dress in your size.
2. Lay the pattern pieces on your chosen fabric, aligning the indicated edge of each piece along the fold of the fabric. Pin them in place, and cut around the perimeter of the pattern pieces. Cut two Dress Front and Back pieces, two Shoulder Strap pieces, and two Front and Back Casing pieces.

Sew Your Dress

3. Place the right sides together of the two Dress Front and Back pieces and stitch up the side seams.
4. Place the right sides of the Front and Back Casing pieces together and sew the short ends together. Fold in half lengthwise, with right sides out, and press.

5. Baste around the top of the dress, gather it to fit the length of the Casing, and pin the Casing in place, with right sides together and raw edges and side seams aligned.
6. With right sides together, fold the Shoulder Strap pieces in half lengthwise. Stitch along the long open edge and one of the short ends. Turn right side out and press.
7. Pin the straps to the Back Casing, each 4" (10cm) from the side seams, lining up the raw edge of the straps with the bottom of the Casing fold. Following the markings on the Casing pattern, pin the left back Strap to the front right of the Casing, and the right back Strap to the left front of the Casing, lining up the raw edges of the Straps with the bottom

of the Casing fold. Since the straps are sewn at an angle, there will be a bit of overlap to trim. It is important to follow the angle on the pattern, so when you cross the two Straps in the front, they will lie at a smooth angle.

8. Starting at one of the side seams, stitch around the bottom of the Casing fold, stitching over the Shoulder Straps and the Dress. Topstitch across each Strap at the top of the Casing to secure the Straps in place. Ⓐ

9. To finish the dress, fold up the hem about ¼" (6mm) and press. Fold another ¼" (6mm), stitch it in place around the entire dress, and press crisp.

Ⓐ

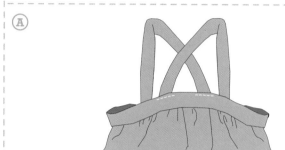

Tie Me Up, Tie Me Down
The Tie Front Strapless Dress

Sometimes an idea is so simple that it gets lost in the mix. But don't let the strapless dress get lost, as it can be worn on any body type, in nearly any fabric, and at any time of year. Completely appropriate for most occasions, this simple strapless dress is made more interesting with a long bow sewn to the front.

Great in soft silk, satin, or lightweight cotton, I chose a black and yellow silk print, with contrasting black for the casing and the long bow. Like other pieces in this collection, there's no need to stick to any rules here. Make the whole thing, including the bow, out of one fabric, or choose different prints for each piece. The choice is yours. Just avoid anything too stiff so that your dress will hang in a flattering way.

FABRIC
2¼ yd (205.7cm) of 45" (114cm) wide, or 1½ yd (137cm) of 60" (152.5cm) wide

NOTIONS
½" (13mm) elastic—Small: 27" (68.5cm); Medium: 29" (74cm); Large: 31" (79cm)

SEAM ALLOWANCE
⅝" (16mm)

TECHNIQUES
Casings and inserting elastic (page 36)

Tie belt (page 30)

Gathering (page 36)

Basting (page 34)

PATTERN PIECES 10 DRESS FRONT AND BACK 01-A FRONT AND BACK CASING (CUT TO 9" [23CM]) 01-A FRONT TIE (CUT TO 22" [56CM])

Cut Out Your Dress

1. Cut out the pattern pieces for the dress in your size.
2. Lay the Dress Front and Back piece on the fold of your chosen fabric, pin it in place, and cut out two pieces around the perimeter of the pattern pieces. Using pattern piece 01-A, cut out four pieces for the Front Tie and two pieces for the Front and Back Casing.

Sew Your Dress

3. Place the right sides of the Dress Front and the Dress Back together and stitch the side seams.
4. With right sides together, sew the short ends of the Casing pieces together. Fold in half lengthwise, with right sides out, and press.

5. Baste around the top of the dress, gather it to fit the length of the Casing, and pin the Casing in place, with right sides together and raw edges and side seams aligned. Starting at one of the side seams, stitch the Casing to the dress, leaving a 1" (2.5cm) opening.

6. Cut the elastic for your desired size. Pin a large safety pin to one end of the elastic, and feed it through the opening in the casing. Be sure not to lose the other end into the bust, and try not to twist the elastic while feeding it through. When you've gone around the whole bust, overlap and pin the two ends of the elastic together. Zigzag stitch the two elastic ends together and close up the hole left in the bust with a straight stitch.

7. To form the Front Tie, with right sides together, sew two of the Front Tie strips together at the short end. Repeat with the other two strips. With these two long strips right sides together, stitch around both short ends and one long edge. Stitch the other long edge, leaving an opening about 2" (5cm) wide. Clip the corners of the seams, turn the tie right side out through the opening, and press crisp. Fold the seam allowance into the opening, press, and slipstitch closed.

8. Fold the dress in half lengthwise to find the center point in the bust Casing, and mark it with a pin. Find and mark the center point of the Front Tie in the same way. Lining up the two center points, pin the Tie to the front of your dress and stitch it in place using a straight stitch, making sure to stitch through the elastic. Ⓐ

9. To finish the dress, fold up the hem about ¼" (6mm) and press. Fold another ¼" (6mm), stitch it in place around the entire dress, and press crisp. Tie the front bow to the desired length.

95

Ⓐ

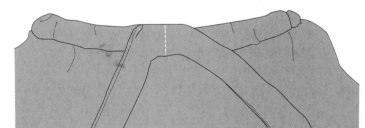

FABRIC

2½ yd (229cm) of 45" (114cm)
wide, or 2½ yd (229cm) of 60"
(152.5cm) wide

SEAM ALLOWANCE

⅝" (16mm)

Wrap It Up
The Wrap Skirt

My entire business began thanks to this skirt. This is the first thing I started to make in a serious way for people to buy. And it sold like hotcakes. Why? Because you can make it in any fabric, and it looks good on every body type. And if you gained five pounds last month, who cares—this skirt will still fit you just fine and look equally amazing. I've also had a handful of customers purchase this skirt who either were expecting a baby or had recently had one. They could wear it through their entire pregnancy (it just slowly got higher and higher on their bodies, and eventually wedged between their belly and bust), and they could wear it immediately after giving birth.

I mean it when I say you can make this in any fabric—corduroy, cotton, silk, wool, whatever. The thicker the fabric, the more severely the skirt will angle out. That's the only difference. To mix it up, try making the waistband tie in a contrasting fabric.

PATTERN PIECES 22 SKIRT 01-A WAIST TIE (CUT TO 18" [45.5CM])

Cut Out Your Skirt

1. Cut out the pattern pieces for the skirt in your size.
2. Lay the pattern pieces on your chosen fabric, aligning the indicated edge of each piece along the fold of the fabric. Pin them in place, and cut around the perimeter of the pattern pieces. Cut out one Skirt piece and two Waist Tie pieces.

Sew Your Skirt

3. Fold the two side edges of the Skirt in about ¼" (6mm) and press. Fold in another ¼" (6mm) and stitch. Press both sides crisp.
4. Fold up the hem about ¼" (6mm) and press. Fold another ¼" (6mm), stitch it in place around the entire Skirt, and press crisp.
5. To form the waistband, stitch the two Waist Tie pieces together, right sides facing, on a short end. Fold in half lengthwise, wrong sides together, and press. Open the fold and fold each half in so the raw edge meets the center fold and press.
6. Find the center point on the Waist Tie and line it up with the center point on the Skirt waist. Pin the Waist Tie in place around the top of the Skirt. Pin along the extra length of the Waist Tie to hold it closed.
7. At each end of the Waist Tie, fold the ends in ½" (13mm) and press. Starting at one end of the Tie, straight stitch along the open edge of the Tie, around the Skirt, and back to the other end of the Tie. Press crisp.

The Finishing Layer
The Jacket

When the air starts to get that crisp autumn chill, you realize that it is time for layers. Not necessarily a parka, but something to top off your T-shirt and jeans. When you are curled up at home on the couch, your fuzzy cable-knit cardigan is just fine. But for that event downtown, this jacket is a great alternative to something boring and shapeless. And like its Trench Coat counterpart (page 57), you can make it without the belt if you so desire.

I picked a deep chocolate brown with cream pearls printed on it. Good fabric choices for the jacket are medium weight cotton, wool, or tweed. If you want to wear the jacket for warmth, you will want something with a bit of substance to it. If you are making it for spring, a lightweight cotton floral will do just fine.

FABRIC
2¼ yd (205.7cm) of 45" (114cm) wide, or 2 yd (183cm) of 60" (152.5cm) wide

NOTIONS
70" (178cm) of handmade bias tape or store-bought ½" (13mm) double-fold bias tape

SEAM ALLOWANCE
⅝" (16mm)

TECHNIQUES
Tie belt (page 30)

Making handmade bias tape (page 39)

Applying bias tape (page 39)

PATTERN PIECES 25 JACKET FRONT 24 JACKET BACK 23 SLEEVE 01-A TIE BELT (OPTIONAL) (CUT AT 18" [45.5CM]) 03 BIAS TAPE (OPTIONAL)

Cut Out Your Jacket

1. Cut out the pattern pieces for the jacket in your size.

2. Lay the pattern pieces on your chosen fabric, aligning the indicated edge of each piece along the fold of the fabric (do not cut the Sleeve or Jacket Front along the fold). Pin them in place, and cut around the perimeter of the pattern pieces. Cut out two Jacket Front pieces, one Jacket Back piece, and two Sleeve pieces. If you would like your jacket to have a belt, cut four Tie Belt pieces.

Sew Your Jacket

3. With right sides together, stitch the front edge of one Sleeve piece (it is marked front) to one Jacket Front piece at the shoulder. Repeat with the other Jacket Front and Sleeve. ⓐ

4. With right sides together, stitch the back edge of one Sleeve piece (marked back) to one Jacket Back piece at the shoulder. Repeat with the other side of the Jacket Back piece.

5. Place the Jacket flat, with the Front and Back facing each other and the Sleeves folded in half, right sides together. Pin up the side seam of the Jacket, under the arm, and down the Sleeve to the cuff. Stitch in place. Repeat on the other side of the Jacket. ⓑ

6. Line up the bias tape you have made or purchased along the front opening of the Jacket on both the left-hand side and the right-hand side, and sew

the tape in place. Pin the bias tape for the neck in place, leaving equal excess tape on both sides. Fold the extra under and pin. Stitch in place.

7. To finish the Jacket, fold up the hem, including the bias tape, about ¼" (6mm), and press. Fold another ¼" (6mm), stitch it in place around the entire jacket, and press crisp. Fold up the cuffs on the Sleeves in the same way and stitch.

8. To make the optional Tie Belt, with right sides together, sew two Tie Belt strips together at a short end. Repeat with the remaining strips. With these two long strips right sides together, stitch both short ends and one long edge. Stitch the other long edge, leaving an opening about 2" (5cm) wide. Clip the corners of the seams, turn the Tie right side out through that opening, and press crisp. Fold the seam allowance into the opening, press, and slipstitch closed.

Ⓑ

Ⓐ

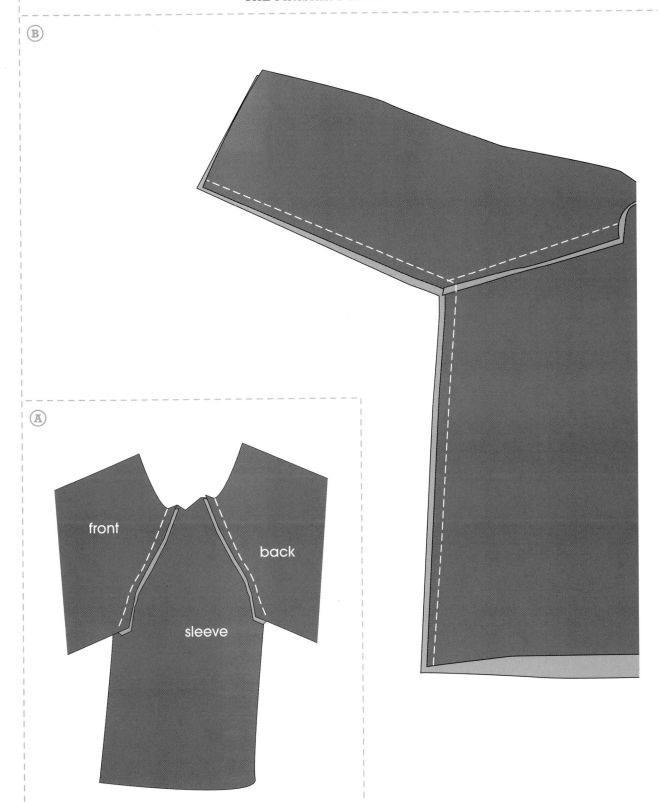

front

back

sleeve

chapter 5

Winter

Winter gets a bad rap. Sure, it can be cold and gray, but it is also the most festive time of year. In what other season can you get away with wearing sequins? Winter is when most parties happen, so you'll need plenty of party dresses.

When the temperatures start to drop, you still need to look good. But since you are a beginning sewer, I have steered away from the serious construction that comes with winter coats and other warm layers. Instead, I went for fun pieces. Included are two party dresses: one with a retro halter and bottom ruffle, and one with a deep plunging V-neck and obi-styled waist belt. I also designed a nightie, a swinging cape, and an adorable shift dress that looks season-appropriate in a back-to-school plaid.

Just as with the clothes for the other seasons in this book, you can get away with these garments in another time of year by changing up the fabric and styling choices. I've just collected them here to help winter's reputation. See, it's not that bad—and it will be spring before you know it.

Show Me What You Got
The Opera Dress

Whether it is for the opera or not, every now and then we all need a fancy dress. This dress has a classic feel with some interesting twists. For example, the sewn-in belt can be tied in a number of ways. In the photos it is pulled to the front first, then wrapped around the back, and then tied in the front on the side in a knot that isn't pulled all the way through. This creates a Japanese obi-style sash. For something more traditional, you can pull it back and tie it in a sweet bow. It's all up to you.

For the fabric, I picked a gorgeous red and ivory silk. For this dress, pick something lightweight, medium weight, or even slightly heavier. Stick to satin, silk, cotton, or blends of those fabric types. Anything too flowy will be too soft at the bust and might cause the wrong thing to be the center of attention.

FABRIC
2½ yd (229cm) of 45" (114cm) wide, or 2 yd (183cm) of 60" (152.5cm) wide

SEAM ALLOWANCE
⅝" (16mm)

TECHNIQUES
Gathering (page 36)

Basting (page 34)

PATTERN PIECES 26 SKIRT FRONT AND BACK 12 BODICE FRONT 11 BODICE BACK 01-B WAIST FRONT (CUT TO 6¾" [17.1CM]) 01-B WAIST BACK (CUT TO 9½" [24CM]) 01-A WAIST TIE (CUT TO 25" [63.5])

Cut Out Your Dress

1. Cut out the pattern pieces for the dress in your size.

2. Lay the pattern pieces on your chosen fabric, aligning the indicated edge of each piece along the fold of the fabric (do not cut the Bodice Front pieces along the fold). Pin them in place, and cut around the perimeter of the pattern pieces. Cut two Skirt Front and Back pieces, two Bodice Back pieces, and four Waist Tie pieces. Cut four Bodice Front pieces, a set of two for the right front and a mirror-image set of two for the left front. Cut one Waist piece at 6¾" (17.1cm) and another Waist piece at 9½" (24cm)—one for the back and one for the front.

Sew Your Dress

3. Place the right sides of the two Skirt Front and Back pieces together and stitch the side seams. Baste around the top of the Skirt and gather it.

4. With right sides together, stitch two of the Waist Tie pieces together along both long edges and one of the short ends, leaving the other short end open. Clip the corners of the seam, turn the Waist Tie right side out, and press flat. Repeat for the remaining two Waist Tie pieces.

5. Place the right sides of the two Waist pieces together. One of the two pieces will buckle under the other, as it is longer. Insert the raw end of one of the Waist Ties between the Waist pieces, aligning

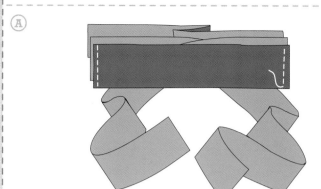

(A)

(B)

106

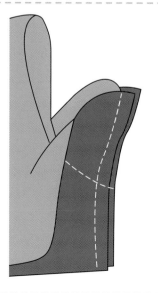

(C)

the Tie's raw end with the Waist pieces' short ends. Center the short end of the tie on the short end of the waist pieces. Pin the Tie in place and stitch the Waist and Tie together along the short end. Repeat to add the remaining Waist Tie to the other side of the Waist. (A)

6. With right sides together and side seams aligned, pin the Waist to the Skirt, adjust the gathering in the Skirt to fit the Waist, and stitch. Be sure to keep the Waist Tie out of the way while sewing.

7. With right sides together, stitch two Bodice Front pieces to one Bodice Back at the shoulder seams. Repeat with the remaining Bodice Front and Back pieces. With right sides together, stitch the Bodice pieces together, stitching up the front, around the neck, and back down the other front side. Then, stitch around each armhole arch. (B) Clip curved seams so that they will lay flat. Turn the entire Bodice right side out and press.

8. Lift the top set of Bodice pieces to face right sides together along the side seam. This creates a straight line down the inside of the side seam. Pin and stitch in place. (C) Lower the Bodice pieces and press. Repeat on other side of Bodice.

9. Overlap the bottom of the Bodice Front sides ¾" (2cm) at the base of the plunging neckline and baste together to hold in place. With right sides facing, pin the Bodice to the Waist and stitch.

10. To finish the dress, hem the Skirt by folding up the bottom about ¼" (6mm) and press. Fold another ¼" (6mm), stitch it in place around the entire dress, and press crisp.

FABRIC

2¾ yd (251.5cm) of
45" (114cm) wide, or
2 yd (183cm) of 60"
(152.5cm) wide

NOTIONS

¼" (6mm) elastic—Small:
12" (30.5cm); Medium: 13½"
(34.5cm); Large: 15" (38cm)

SEAM ALLOWANCE

⅝" (16mm)

TECHNIQUES

Gathering (page 36)

Basting (page 34)

Casings and inserting elastic
(page 36)

Patch pockets (page 35)

Hot For Teacher
The Back-to-School Shift Dress

When the weather starts to get chilly, I become excited about one print you just can't pull off in the heat of the summer—plaids. Sure, you can wear this dress in other prints, but there's something so adorable about this garment in plaid. And it allows you to make the pockets on the diagonal to create that great contrast.

I chose a black, white, gray, and hot pink plaid that has a classic yet girly feel. Pick what you like, but this pattern works best with lightweight fabric. That can be as diverse as wool, cotton, silk, or even a lightweight corduroy. Top it with a cardigan or hoodie, slip on some tights and a pair of boots, and it will be just like your co-ed days.

PATTERN PIECES 09 DRESS FRONT 08 DRESS BACK 13 FRONT NECK BAND 14 BACK NECK BAND
31 SLEEVE 16 POCKET (OPTIONAL)

Cut Out Your Dress

1. Cut out the pattern pieces for the dress in your size.

2. Lay the pattern pieces on your chosen fabric, aligning the indicated edge of each piece along the fold of the fabric (do not cut the Sleeve pieces along the fold). Pin them in place, and cut around the perimeter of the pattern pieces. Cut one Dress Front piece, one Dress Back piece, two Sleeve pieces, two Front Neck Band pieces, and two Back Neck Band pieces. One set of Neck Band pieces will be the Neck Band Facing, which will be on the inside of the dress. Cut two Pockets if you are putting pockets on your shift.

Sew Your Dress

3. Place the right sides of the Dress Front and the Dress Back together and stitch the side seams. Fold the Sleeve in half crosswise, right sides together, and stitch the two short ends together. Turn the Sleeve right side out. Hold the dress with the wrong side out and an armhole facing you. Pin the Sleeve to the Dress at the armhole, lining up the top of the Sleeve with the top of the Dress Front and the Dress Back. Stitch in place. Repeat for the other Sleeve. Baste around the entire top of the dress, including the Sleeves, and gather. Ⓐ

4. With right sides together, stitch the Front Neck Band to the Back Neck Band at both short ends. Repeat for the Neck Band Facing. Lining up the seams,

Ⓐ

110

place the right sides of the Neck Band and the Neck Band Facing together, and stitch around the inner circle. Clip curved seams, turn the Facing to the inside, wrong sides together, and press. Baste the two layers together around the outer circle.

5. Pin the Neck Band to the Dress, right sides together, aligning the side seams in the Neck Band with the centers of the Sleeves. Adjust the Sleeve, Dress Front, and Dress Back gathers to fit, and stitch the Neck Band in place.

6. Fold the bottom of one Sleeve under about ¼" (6mm) and press. Fold under again about ½" (13mm) and press again. Stitch around the top of the fold, leaving a 1" (2.5cm) opening near the seam where you started. Cut the elastic for your desired size. Pin a large safety pin to one end of the

elastic, and feed it through the casing. Be sure not to lose the other end into the Sleeve, and try not to twist the elastic while feeding it through. When you've gone around the whole Sleeve, overlap and pin the ends together. Zigzag stitch the two elastic ends together and close up the hole left in the Sleeve with a straight stitch. Repeat for the other Sleeve.

7. To make the optional Pockets, follow the instructions in the techniques section (page 35). Place the Pocket pieces on the Dress, following the markings on the Dress Front pattern piece, and sew them in place.

8. To finish the Dress, fold up the hem about ¼" (6mm) and press. Fold another ¼" (6mm), stitch it in place around the entire Dress, and press crisp.

FABRIC
3¼ yd (297.2cm) of
45" (114cm) wide, or
2¼ yd (205.7cm) of
60" (152.5cm) wide

NOTIONS
½" (13mm) elastic for bust—
Small: 27" (68.5cm); Medium:
29" (74cm); Large: 31" (79cm)

½" (13mm) elastic for
waist—Small: 25" (63.5cm);
Medium: 27" (68.5cm);
Large: 29" (74cm)

SEAM ALLOWANCE
⅝" (16mm)

TECHNIQUES
Casings and inserting elastic
(page 36)

Be a Modern Marilyn
The Halter Dress

It's that time of year when you are going to holiday parties, cocktail parties, and of course, a New Year's Eve party. Sure, it might be cold, but really, are you going to wear long sleeves and pants? I don't think so. You're going to wear something amazing.

I wanted to play up the pinup feel of this halter, so I chose to make it in light gray and black polka dot silk. It is classic and elegant but also fun and sexy. This dress is great on most body types, and can be made in anything soft and flowy. Lightweight cotton, silk, satin, and rayon are really the best choices. And you can make the ruffle out of whatever you like, or skip it completely. It's your party, so do what you want.

PATTERN PIECES **26** SKIRT FRONT AND BACK **30** BODICE FRONT **29** BODICE BACK
01-A HALTER TIE (CUT AT 25" [63.5CM]) **02** RUFFLE

111

Cut Out Your Dress

1. Cut out the pattern pieces for the dress in your size.
2. Lay the pattern pieces on your chosen fabric, aligning the indicated edge of each piece along the fold of the fabric. Pin them in place, and cut around the perimeter of the pattern pieces. Cut two Skirt Front and Back pieces, one Bodice Front piece, one Bodice Back piece, two Ruffle pieces, and two Halter Tie pieces.

Sew Your Dress

3. Place the right sides of the two Skirt Front and Back together and stitch up the side seams.
4. With right sides of the Bodice Front and Bodice Back together, sew up the two side seams. Fold down the

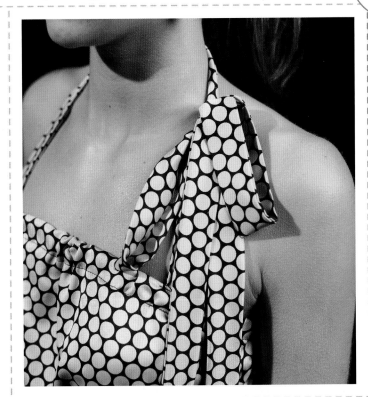

top of the Bodice ¼" (6mm) and press. Fold again about 1" (2.5cm) and press.

5. With right sides together, fold both Halter Tie pieces in half lengthwise. Stitch along the long edge and one of the short ends. Turn right side out and press.

6. Pin the Ties to the Bodice Front, each 4" (10cm) from one of the side seams, lining up the raw edge of the Ties with the bottom of the casing fold.

7. Starting at one of the side seams, stitch around the bottom of the casing fold, stitching over the two Ties and leaving a 1" (2.5cm) opening at the seam where you started. Before inserting the elastic, straight stitch across each Tie at the top of the

Bodice to secure the Ties in place. Be careful to stitch close to the folded edge in order to leave enough space for the elastic to go through the casing. Ⓐ

8. Cut the elastic for your desired bust size. Pin a large safety pin to one end of the elastic, and feed it through the casing. Be sure not to lose the other end, and try not to twist the elastic while feeding it through. When you've gone around the bust, overlap and pin the two ends together. Zigzag stitch the two elastic ends together and close up the hole left in the Bodice with a straight stitch.

9. With right sides together, pin the bottom of the Bodice to the top of the Skirt, lining up the side seams in the Skirt with the side seams in the Bodice. Stitch 1¼" (3cm) below the edge where the Skirt and Bodice meet. Stitch again ½" (2cm) below the edge, leaving a 1" (2.5cm) opening at the Bodice side seam where you started.

10. Cut the elastic for your desired waist size and insert it to the waist casing as you did for the bust.

11. To make the bottom Ruffle, place the right sides of the two Ruffle pieces together and sew the two short ends together. Turn the ruffle right side out. Baste around one of the long sides and gather to match the circumference of the bottom of the Skirt. Pin in place, line up side seams, right sides facing, and stitch.

12. To finish the dress, hem the Ruffle by folding up the bottom about ¼" (6mm) and press. Fold another ¼" (6mm), stitch it in place around the entire Ruffle, and press crisp.

Ⓐ

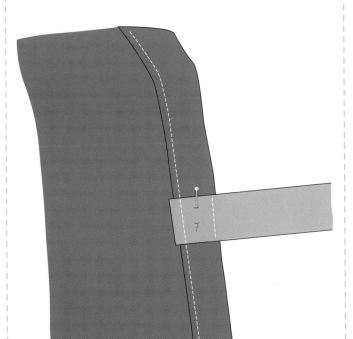

113

French Kissing
The Nightie

It doesn't matter whether you're single or married: Everyone needs a sexy nightie. You don't need overnight company to treat yourself to something nice. In fact, it can make you feel even more luxurious if you put it on for no special reason when you are home alone. Don't you want to be one of those women who drinks martinis in lingerie while watching television, even if you're alone? I know I do!

For this nightie, I chose a beautiful aqua blue satin with a cream lace. Of course, you can go crazy and choose whatever fabric you like. Make it in a satin, a silk, or a lightweight cotton, and the results will be the same. The lace you choose can be any width, as long as it is flat and not gathered or ruffled.

FABRIC
1¾ yd (160cm) of 45" (114cm) wide, or 1 yd (91cm) of 60" (152.5cm) wide

NOTIONS
Flat lace for straps—Small: 32" (81cm); Medium: 36" (91cm); Large: 40" (101.5cm)

Flat lace for bust—Small: 36" (91cm); Medium: 38" (96.5cm); Large; 40" (101.6cm)

Flat lace for hem—Small: 50" (127cm); Medium: 51" (129.5cm); Large: 52" (132.1cm)

SEAM ALLOWANCE
⅝" (16mm)

TECHNIQUES
Attaching lace (page 37)

Seam finishing (page 34)

Gathering (page 36)

Basting (page 34)

PATTERN PIECES 10 DRESS FRONT AND BACK

Cut Out Your Nightie

1. Cut out the pattern piece for the nightie in your size.
2. Lay out the Dress Front and Back piece on the fold of the lingerie fabric and cut out two pieces around the perimeter of the pattern. Satin and silks are slippery and move a lot while cutting, so be sure to use weights to keep the pattern pieces in place while cutting. If you are going to use pins, test one in a corner first, as silk sometimes doesn't recover well from those little holes.

Sew Your Nightie

3. Zigzag stitch around the top and bottom of each piece to keep it from fraying.
4. Cut the strip of lace for the hem in half crosswise. With the wrong side of lace facing the right side of the fabric, pin one half in place on the Dress Front and one on the Dress Back, with about ½" (13mm) of lace overlapping the fabric. Using a zigzag stitch, attach the lace to the bottom of the two nightie pieces. Ⓐ

5. Switch back to a straight stitch and, with right sides together, sew the front and the back of the nightie together along both sides. Turn the nightie right side out.

6. Baste along the top of the nightie and gather the edge. With right sides together, sew the lace for the bust strip's ends together. Pin the wrong side of the lace to the top of the right side of the nightie, overlapping the lace about ½" (13mm) as you did on the hem, adjust the gathering to fit, and zigzag stitch the lace in place.

7. Cut the strip of lace for the straps in half crosswise. Pin one end of each strap to the inside top of the nightie front, with the center of your chosen lace 4" (10cm) from each side seam. Line up the bottom of the lace with the zigzag stitch on the top of the nightie. Pin the remaining ends of the straps to the back of the nightie, aligning them, again, to the stitch at the top of the nightie. Zigzag stitch the straps in place along the zigzag that holds the lace trim to the nightie top. Also zigzag stitch across the strap at the top of the nightie lace to secure it in place. B

116

A
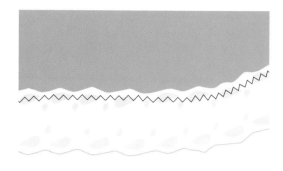

B
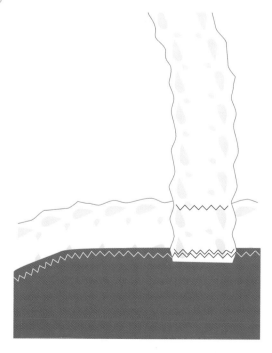

Be a Superhero
The Cape

The cape has always been a chic and timeless layer. Great over jeans and a T-shirt, a cocktail dress, and everything in between, this shape is appropriate for everyone, all the time. One place you've probably seen the cape is on actresses in films from the 1940s. You know, the ones who are always described as having gumption. Those ladies always seemed to have a level of self-confidence that I admire. But why just admire them, when you can be them?

For this cape I chose a medium weight black-and-white wool. The key to this garment is that it hangs and flows smoothly. You don't want to choose any fabric that is too heavy or too stiff. Wool is a great choice, as is polyester crepe, which has the shine of a fancy fabric but is stronger than traditional polyester. You can even make the cape with silk and add rhinestone buttons for a formal occasion.

FABRIC
2½ yd (229cm) of 45" (114cm) wide, or 2½ yd (229cm) of 60" (152.5cm) wide

NOTIONS
37" (94cm) length of ½" (13mm) double-fold bias tape, purchased or handmade

2 flat buttons of your choice

SEAM ALLOWANCE
⅝" (16mm)

TECHNIQUES
Making handmade bias tape (page 39)

Applying bias tape (page 39)

Sewing on buttons (page 38)

117

PATTERN PIECES 22 CAPE 03 BIAS TAPE (OPTIONAL)

Cut Out Your Cape

1. Cut out the pattern pieces for the cape in your size.

2. Fold the fabric crosswise instead of selvage-to-selvage. Lay the Cape piece on the fold of your fabric, pin it in place, and cut one piece out around the perimeter of the pattern piece. If you choose to make bias tape, use pattern piece 03 and follow the directions in the Techniques section (page 39).

Sew Your Cape

3. Fold the neckline down ¼" (6mm) and press. Fold another ¼" (6mm) down and stitch along the neckline near the bottom fold. Fold the bottom

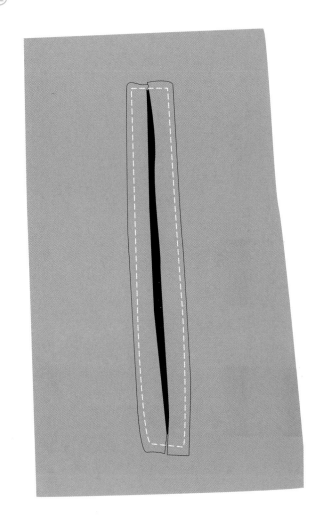

Ⓐ

hem up ¼" (6mm) and press. Then, fold another ¼" (6mm) up and stitch along the hem near the top fold. Fold the side edges in ¼" (6mm) and press. Then fold another ¼" (6mm) in and stitch the sides near the inner fold.

4. Following the lines on the pattern piece, carefully cut a slit on each side for armholes. A rotary cutter makes this much easier.

5. Cut the bias tape into four strips of 9¼" (23.5cm). Open the center fold of the tape, fold in ¼" (6mm) on each end, and press—this will keep the raw end of the bias tape concealed. Repeat for the remaining three bias tape strips.

6. Pin one bias tape strip to each side of one armhole slit and stitch along the strips' length, near the open side of the tape. After stitching the strips in place, stitch each end to secure them. Repeat on the other armhole slit. Ⓐ

7. Overlap the sides of the Cape at the top by 5" (12.5cm) and pin. Measure in about 1" (2.5cm) from the front sides, mark with a pin, and sew your chosen buttons in place through both layers.

Glossary

Backstitching To finish off a seam, put your machine in reverse for a few stitches, and then continue moving forward.

Basting stitch A straight stitch, longer and looser than a normal stitch, that is meant to hold two pieces together temporarily.

Bias True bias is the 45-degree angle against the grain of a woven fabric. This is where fabric stretches the most.

Bobbin One of the two threads when making a stitch is stored in the bobbin, which is located under the needle and throat plates on your sewing machine.

Casing A channel created when fabric is folded and stitched, through which elastic or some other closing material is fed.

Gathering To fit a wider amount of fabric into a smaller space by pulling the threads tight.

Grain The threads in a fabric that run parallel to the selvage.

Grainline arrow A pattern marking that indicates which way the piece should be placed on the fabric relative to the grain of the fabric.

Hem The end of the garment at its longest point. The bottom of a dress, or the bottom of a top, for example.

Nap Fabrics that have one direction in which they should be used.

Notches Triangular chunks cut out of curved seams that help the seams lie flat.

One-way prints Printed fabrics with designs that go in a specific direction, like a plaid, or a floral, where the flowers move in the same direction.

One-way fabrics Fabrics that have a direction or nap, like corduroy, which has a brushed surface that goes in one direction.

Right side The front of the fabric that is worn on the outside of the body and is meant to be seen.

Seam allowance The amount of fabric between the stitching of a seam and the raw edge of the fabric. For the projects in this book, the seam allowance is 5/8" (16mm).

Seam Where two pieces of fabric are sewn together on a garment.

Selvage When you buy fabric, the top and bottom edges of the fabric are finished off in the manufacturing process. Those finished edges are the selvage.

Topstitch Used usually for decorative detail, topstitching is stitching done on the right side, or the outside, of a garment.

Wrong side The inside of the fabric that is worn next to the body and is not meant to be seen.

Zigzag A stitch made on a sewing machine in zigzag mode. The thread moves back and forth in a Z pattern and is used when making buttonholes, attaching trim, or finishing seams.

Resources

All of the projects in this book call for materials that are readily available at fabric stores near you. The following list of suppliers will help you find all the materials you need to complete the projects in this book. If you have trouble finding a product, consult the websites listed to locate a distributor near you.

FABRIC

HANCOCK FABRICS

Nationwide retailers

877-322-7427

www.HancockFabrics.com

MICHAEL LEVINE FABRICS

920 Maple Avenue, Los Angeles, CA 90015

213-622-6259

www.MLFabric.com

MOOD FABRICS

225 West 37th Street, 3rd Floor, New York, NY 10018

212-730-5003

6151 West Pico Boulevard, Los Angeles, CA 90035

323-653-6663

www.MoodFabrics.com

REPRODEPOT FABRICS

Online only

413-527-4047

www.ReproDepot.com

VOGUE FABRICS

718–732 Main Street, Evanston, IL 60202

623–627 West Roosevelt Road, Chicago, IL 60607

16919 Torrence Avenue, Lansing, IL 60438

800-433-4313

www.VogueFabricsStore.com

NOTIONS

FRED FRANKEL & SONS

19 West 38th Street, New York, NY 10018

212-840-0810

www.FredFrankel.com

JO-ANN FABRIC AND CRAFT STORES

Nationwide locations

888-739-4120

www.JoAnn.com

M&J TRIMMING

1008 Sixth Avenue, New York, NY 10018

800-965-8746

www.MJTrim.com

MICHAELS

8000 Bent Branch Dr.

Irving, TX 75063

800-642-4235

www.Michaels.com

HARDWARE AND TOOLS

BERNINA

Worldwide Retailers

630-978-2500

www.Bernina.com

BROTHER

Worldwide retailers

877-276-8437

www.Brother-USA.com/HomeSewing

HUSQVARNA VIKING

Worldwide retailers

800-358-0001

www.HusqvarnaViking.com

PFAFF SEWING MACHINES

Worldwide retailers

800-997-3233

www.PfaffUSA.com

SINGER SEWING COMPANY

Worldwide retailers

800-474-6437

www.SingerCO.com

VECCHIARELLI BROTHERS, INC.

121 West 15th Street, Los Angeles, CA 90015

213-749-5944

www.VEBros.com

123

ACKNOWLEDGMENTS

It took so many people to make this book happen. I'd like to send a special thanks to the following people: to the ladies at Random House—Melissa Bonventre, without whom this book would never have been conceived in the first place; Jennifer Graham, who supported me along the way; and Amy Sly, who made my manuscript so beautiful; to my tech editor Kevin Kosbab, for helping my words make sense; to the mind-reading and mind-blowing photo team of Stuart Mullenberg and Chris Bennett; to Rena Leinberger for her charming illustrations; to Kent Bell, who helped me secure the deal with his beautifully designed proposal; to the lovely models—Annabelle Waters, Tessa Young, and Liz Russo—for working long and hard hours; and to Carla Sinclair, who published the article that lead to this book. A big thanks to Laura Howe for allowing me to photograph at her store, Matrushka, and to Michael Hampton and the team at Ford's Filling Station for letting us interrupt their brunch setup with our photo shoot.

On a personal note, there are a few people to thank for helping me along this journey. My mom and my late father, without whose love and support I could not have done any of this; Michael McCurry, who always reminds me of who I am; and my amazing friends Ileana Rodriguez, Jenifer Lake, Leah Heisel, and Jennifer Seigle, who are a constant source of inspiration, love, and support.

ABOUT THE AUTHOR

Christine Haynes was born in Detroit and learned to sew from her mother (who learned from her mother before her). Christine graduated from the School of the Art Institute of Chicago, and it was while in Chicago that she first launched her clothing label, then called Twospace. While at first she focused on one-of-a-kind, highly conceptual pieces to be sold at indie craft fairs, the line soon made a natural shift to the modern and wearable aesthetic that remains at the heart of the company today.

Christine's eponymous clothing line, Christine Haynes, is sold in specialty boutiques around the world. London, Honolulu, Chicago, New York, San Francisco, Los Angeles, Milwaukee, and Philadelphia top the list of cities where her pieces are available. Christine's work has been featured in *The New York Times, The New York Post, Los Angeles Times, Time Out London,* MSNBC.com, People.com, *LA Weekly, Venus* magazine, *Daily Candy,* and the *Today* Show, among others. To learn more about Christine or to see her line, visit her at www.ChristineHaynes.com.

Index

Milieu du dos—Placez cette ligne sur le pli